Employment, Unemployment, and Health Insurance:

Behavioral and Descriptive Analysis of Health Insurance Loss Due to Unemployment

A. James Lee

Abt Books
Cambridge, Massachusetts

This book is based on material prepared for the National Center for Health Services Research under Contract No. HRA 230-75-0128. The findings expressed here are those of the author and do not necessarily reflect the views of the National Center for Health Services Research.

Library of Congress Catalog Card Number 78-66689

© Abt Associates Inc., 1979

Printed in the United States of America.

ISBN: 0-89011-516-8

Contents

Tables and Figures

Acknowledgments

Possibly the most enjoyable part of an author's task is thanking the many people who helped along the way and who consequently share credit for the completed work. Of course, the author alone assumes full liability for mistakes and shortcomings.

First, I wish to thank the National Center for Health Services Research (NCHSR) for supporting this research project, which was one of several examining the impact of the business cycle on access to health care. I especially wish to thank NCHSR Project Officers Ira Raskin and James Daugherty for their patience in contending with a first-time project director. Furthermore, without the intellectual freedom allowed by them this study would not have been worth nearly as much to the taxpayers who have paid for it.

Most of all, I wish to thank Dr. Frank A. Sloan of Vanderbilt University. Frank and Dr. Jerry Cromwell, Abt Associates Inc. (AAI), provided the initial impetus for this study that I inherited on coming to AAI. The at-risk analysis was Frank's idea. In addition, Frank has monitored and guided progress throughout the study and has given thoughtful comments on Chapters 2, 3, and 4, as well as the appendix.

I am also indebted to Drs. Howard Birnbaum and Douglas Wilson (AAI) for in-house review and comment. Doug was especially helpful in shaping the first part of Chapter 2.

I wish to thank Drs. Ronald Andersen and Lu Ann Aday (Center for Hospital Administration Studies) for making their newly completed medical access study available to me for analysis. Roger Reynold programmed this very useful data source in Chicago.

Larry Kanarek did the programming in Cambridge, with an occasional assist from James Gokhale and Michael Schwartz. Larry also read chapter drafts and contributed many useful insights.

Dr. Susan Windham (AAI) prepared a very early draft of Chapter 3 and some of her insights remain in the present chapter. She also assisted me with other aspects of the study.

Ellen Sward has edited most of the manuscript. The report is much improved by her efforts. She exhibited an uncanny ability to ferret out ambiguities of meaning and prompt me to think again.

Finally, I wish to thank Georgette Wright for patiently typing the various chapter drafts and supervising production of the final manuscript.

A. James Lee
Cambridge, Massachusetts

1

Introduction: An Overview and Summary

BACKGROUND

On February 17, 1975, in the midst of the 1974–75 recession, the AFL-CIO Executive Council issued the following statement:

There are now 7.5 million unemployed workers in the United States, 8.2 percent of the labor force.

According to the Library of Congress more than 80 percent of the workers laid off during 1974 lost their health insurance coverage. A survey of health insurance contracts indicates at least two out of three workers have no health insurance after being unemployed for one month or more. Thus, if unemployed workers wish to continue their health insurance after coverage is terminated they must pay the premium, usually at exorbitant individual rates, at a time when they are financially pressed and least able to do so.

Stripped of their group coverage and denied Medicaid because they are not poor enough, a serious illness in the family could leave some unemployed workers bankrupt. Many will postpone needed medical care for themselves and their families because they won't be able to pay sky-high doctor bills with meager unemployment insurance checks. This situation is intolerable and would not have existed had Congress enacted National Health Security which provides health benefits for all residents whether they are employed or unemployed. [1]

1

Although the AFL-CIO was not the only organization concerned with health insurance for the unemployed, its statement quickly introduces the nature of the problem and illustrates the intensity of that concern. Approximately 80 percent of nonelderly persons in the United States have some kind of private health insurance. The vast majority of this health insurance is purchased through an employer to take advantage of substantial group discounts in the "price" of health insurance. Though this linkage of health insurance to employment is convenient and inexpensive as long as one remains employed, it is not so convenient and inexpensive when one becomes unemployed. Even though many employment-related group health insurance plans provide for conversion to individually purchased policies, the cost disadvantage is significant. Individual or nongroup health insurance costs 70 to 80 percent more than equivalent group health insurance, presumably because of the greater marketing and administrative costs of such policies. In addition, the unemployed individual must pay the entire premium, whereas most employers pay a large share or all of it. Finally, individual premiums are customarily paid quarterly rather than the monthly norm for group health insurance, further compounding the financial burden at time of payment. Of course, unemployed workers and their families have also suffered large, short-term reductions in current income and typically must severely limit their standard of living, often by making difficult choices among such necessities as food, housing, clothing, education, and medical care.

When the 1974–75 recession, the steepest economic decline since the Great Depression, bottomed out in May 1975, 9.2 percent of workers were unemployed—a total of 8.4 million. For many the loss of employment meant losing not only income but also job-related group health insurance. The seeming enormity of the health insurance problem prompted congressional interest in the possibility of extending health insurance protection to the unemployed, a step that would have been the most significant expansion of federally sponsored medical benefits in the last decade. Not since the advent of Medicaid in 1965 had Congress moved to extend health benefits to as large a group as the unemployed.[2] At least four congressional committees held public hearings on the issue, receiving supportive testimony from a host of interested parties (such as the AFL-CIO, UAW, Blue Cross Association, American Medical Association, and American Hospital Association). Various bills were introduced that would have extended "emergency" health insurance benefits to the unemployed. However, the Ford administration strongly opposed such legislation and the proposals died in committee as the recession ended and the recovery ensued.

Even though congressional and other interest has now apparently flagged, the problem of health insurance loss during unemployment has not disappeared, although it persists at a somewhat lower level. The purpose of this study has been to advance our understanding of health insurance loss by the unemployed and to provide a more complete factual basis for responding to it in the future, either as an ongoing problem or as it becomes aggravated by subsequent recession. In addition, this study has much to add to the ongoing discussion of national health insurance. It has generated considerable up-to-date information on health insurance, both among the unemployed and the employed.

THE ANALYTIC QUESTIONS

It is often useful to divide the relevant questions to be asked into two categories: *normative* and *positive.* Normative questions relate to "what should be" whereas positive questions concern "what is." In the context of this study the key normative question is whether the loss of health insurance by the unemployed warrants government intervention. Is it desirable that the government extend health insurance protection to the unemployed; or, equivalently, do the social and economic benefits of such a government program exceed the costs? Unfortunately, this crucial normative question cannot be easily answered; although I attempt to illuminate various considerations, the present state of the art does not permit even a tentative conclusion. The positive questions are much more readily answered and receive the greatest attention in this study.

The positive questions concern the extent, kind, and distribution of health insurance lost by the unemployed; the extent to which existing public programs such as Medicaid mitigate the consequences of private health insurance loss; the behavioral determinants of health insurance loss; and the like. These questions concern what actually happens—or as a corollary what might happen—if various emergency health insurance alternatives were enacted. How many persons would be affected? What would the cost be? The answers to these relatively simply factual questions may help to shape the answer to the more fundamental normative questions. Furthermore, if the normative question is answered affirmatively—that is, if government provided health insurance for the unemployed is desirable—the factual data can facilitate the design and orderly introduction of an appropriate policy response.

SUMMARY OF EMPIRICAL FINDINGS

I have used both cross-tabular and multivariate procedures to investigate the impact of unemployment on the demand for and access to health insurance. Though the cross-tabular studies give a more descriptive appraisal of the problem—that is, the extent, kind and distribution of health insurance lost—the multivariate studies give a more behavioral analysis—an understanding of the underlying causal factors. Both have important implications for the development of public policy. However, they answer fundamentally different questions and should not be viewed as substitutes for one another, but rather as complements.

Cross-Tabular or Descriptive Investigation

Three separate descriptive studies have been conducted. (1) We tabulate private health insurance coverage parameters—such as covered services, deductibles, and maximum payments, as well as the simple existence of health insurance—by employment status (employed or unemployed) to make inferences about the extent and kind of health insurance lost due to unemployment. The health insurance coverages are tabulated from four different data sources, each of which is a national probability sample. (2) We investigate the distribution of health insurance losses due to unemployment. We do this by tabulating demographic-specific health insurance coverage rates for the employed and unemployed and taking the difference between them as an estimate for the impact of unemployment. In this way the characteristics of those persons who are most (or least) likely to lose health insurance due to loss of employment can be determined. (3) We investigate whether and how well Medicaid substitutes for private health insurance lost due to unemployment.[3] We do this, in part, by tabulating the sources of payment for family health care—including Medicaid—by employment status of the household head.

The leading findings from these descriptive studies may be briefly summarized:

Our most recent data source indicates that private health insurance enrollment rates among the unemployed are 29 to 35 percentage points lower than enrollment rates among employed persons. If we divide these figures by the percentage of employed persons with health insurance, we find that 35 to 39 percent of those with health insurance when employed lost it when they became unemployed.

We estimate that during the 1974–75 recession between 875,000 and 1,071,000 households had lost health insurance at any one time because of the unemployment of the household head.

The level of health insurance among the unemployed has increased sharply during the 1970s.

No more than 10–14 percent of workers losing group health insurance have substituted individual nongroup health insurance.

The "quality" of health insurance lost by the unemployed is somewhat lower but not too much different from the average.

Health insurance losses are not evenly distributed across the various demographic and socioeconomic groups. The probability of health insurance loss is greatest for young workers, nonwhite workers, unmarried workers, female workers, workers with large families, low-income workers, workers living in central cities, workers not living in the North Central region, and workers in selected occupations and industries. The probability of health insurance loss did not vary significantly with education or health status.

Households in which the spouse works have a seven percentage point lower probability of health insurance loss due to unemployment of the head. Dividing this figure by the percentage probability of health insurance loss in the larger population, we estimate that the probability of losing health insurance is reduced by 27 percent.

Not surprisingly, the probability of health insurance loss varies directly with the duration of unemployment. The "structurally" unemployed are much more likely to lose health insurance.

Between 19 and 31 percent of the unemployed without private health insurance receive health care from Medicaid and related sources. Another 10 to 18 percent receive at least some health care from sources like the V.A. and workmen's compensation. Between 51 and 71 percent of the unemployed without private health insurance have no public health insurance alternatives whatsoever.

The unemployed who are not eligible for Medicaid pay 60 percent of health care costs out of pocket, compared to 14 percent for Medicaid-eligibles. Furthermore, the health care expenditure by the Medicaid-eligible unemployed is over twice as much as for those not eligible.

The low-income employed have even less health insurance protection than do the unemployed, above or below the poverty level.

Multivariate or Behavioral Investigation

Recall that multivariate procedures were used to analyze the loss of health insurance due to unemployment and to isolate those factors that, in addition to employment itself, influence the magnitude of health insurance coverage.

We began by examining the theoretic context of health insurance loss by the unemployed. Because the theory of health insurance has received much attention in recent years we did not pursue a fully comprehensive discussion of the underlying theoretic model. Instead we gave special attention to several theoretic considerations that are especially relevant to this study. (1) We suggested that previous analyses of the effect of income on the demand for health insurance do not generalize to the large and transitory income reductions associated with loss of employment and that it was necessary to estimate a transitory income elasticity (or effect) for assessing the impact of job loss, and associated income loss, on the demand for health insurance. (2) We also suggested that continuation of group health insurance by the former employer is significant and that loss of group health insurance by the unemployed is not fully arbitrary or capricious but rather reflects underlying economic factors. That is, we suggested that unemployed workers continue to demand health insurance from their previous employer and that these unemployed worker demands partly determine the extent of continuation. While this prospect seemed counterintuitive, it has become more credible given recent understanding of the importance of temporary layoffs in the theory of the firm.

We used data from 1970, 1972, and 1975–76 to estimate group and nongroup health insurance demand relationships. In most cases the health insurance demands were estimated separately for the employed and the unemployed to allow for interaction between work status and the other independent variables. The estimation strongly supported our hypothesis that unemployed workers continue to demand group health insurance from their previous employer. In particular, continuation of group health insurance durng unemployment was shown to be systematically (and significantly) related to the economic variables—income and price—as well as to the other demographic characteristics.

The quantitive importance of continuation is, however, another matter. Only a small fraction—between 5 and 25 percent—of actual health insurance loss by the unemployed could be explained by our modeling effort. After considering several alternative explanations, we concluded that many unemployed workers simply do not have the opportunity to continue group health insurance from their former employer. Either the employer is insensitive to the demands for continuation of health insurance during unemployment, or the employed workers themselves are insensitive to the prospect of unemployment and fail to transmit their "true" demands by negotiating continuation of group health insurance during unemployment as part of the terms of their employment. Thus, the level of health insurance among the unemployed may be inefficiently too low (or suboptimal), assuming that the employer's group price in fact represents the social cost of continuing the insurance. That is, we attribute much of the unemployment-related reduction in health insurance to a health insurance market failure. The reduction seems to be largely an artifact of the predominant work-group institutional mechanism for financing health insurance in our country and may bear little or no relation to underlying demand and cost considerations.

Also, an employed worker's likelihood of having health insurance depends substantially on the industry of employment, even after controlling for demographic and other relevant characteristics of the worker. That is, the provision of health insurance to the employed also depends importantly on institutional arrangements unrelated to demand variation. In addition, we found that a self-employed worker is much less likely to have group health insurance than an otherwise similar nonself-employed worker, and that a female or nonwhite head of household is less likely to have group health insurance than an otherwise similar male or white head of household. We also found that, contrary to expectations, those with "poor" health have a lesser likelihood of having health insurance than those with average health. This finding may reflect institutional barriers to the acquisition of health insurance by such persons—

so-called uninsurables or high-risk persons. That is, a health insurance market for this population may not exist.

We estimate that the expected value of benefits from health insurance is about 10 percent less for the unemployed than for otherwise similar employed persons. This supports our conclusion from the descriptive work that the quality of health insurance lost due to unemployment is not too much different from the average.

We have also briefly explored—as a digression—the impact of unemployment on the demand for health care. The results were surprising. Contrary to empirical tradition, we found that health insurance does not lead to an increase in the utilization of health care services by the general population. However, health insurance increases health care expense by $485 per year in households where the head is unemployed. Although it is premature to draw conclusions until alternative explanations can be investigated and the analysis can be replicated from other sources, the results have a variety of interesting implications.

First, the "moral hazard" associated with health insurance does not appear to influence the health care demands of the larger working population. Apparently, families with the head employed have sufficient income to purchase the desired level of health services and health insurance does not bias toward overuse. Previous findings suggesting the contrary may reflect failure to control for employment status. Second, the finding that health insurance is important for the unemployed tends to indicate that inability to borrow against future income—a financial market failure—is the cause of the reduced health care expenditure by the unemployed not having health insurance and that such reduction is inefficient. However, this inference remains substantially speculative at this stage. Nevertheless, we believe that our findings demand a reexamination of the now-conventional wisdom that health insurance leads to overutilization of health services. Our results are more nearly consistent with the view that it corrects underutilization.

Finally, we have used our results from analyzing the 1975–76 data to simulate cyclical variation in the extent of health insurance lost due to unemployment. Health insurance loss by the unemployed had been perceived as being merely a recessionary problem. However, the simulation demonstrates that the problem persists, albeit at a lower level, even in time of economic well-being. In particular, the results suggest that the extent of health insurance loss during the 1974–75 recession was no more than twice as large as it would be during typical nonrecession years.

PUBLIC POLICY IMPLICATIONS

We also have examined our findings more explicitly in the context of the public policy concerns surrounding the loss of health insurance by the unemployed. In particular, we have explored the implications of various alternatives for extending health insurance to the unemployed. We discuss the various emergency health insurance programs that were proposed as federal legislation at the time of the 1974–75 recession and set out some of the criteria that should be used in evaluating them. While we do not attempt a rigorous evaluation of the proposals, we use our empirical findings to formulate some of the policy issues presented by the various proposals.

In addition, we recommend a nongovernmental alternative that may solve much or most of the health insurance loss problem. In particular, we suggest that insurers and employers permit continuation of group health insurance from a former employer so long as the unemployed worker pays its true social cost.[4] This cost would include the full health insurance premium amount paid by the employer to the insurer (including any portion formerly paid by the employer) plus any costs borne by the employer in continuing the health insurance—for example, the costs of collecting the premium and providing assistance with claims. If continuation were offered on this basis, neither the employer nor the insurer would be worse off and yet unemployed workers who could purchase health insurance at something approaching the group rate—assuming that the employer costs are minimal—would be better off. Our empirical findings suggest that such a social innovation would reduce present health insurance losses of the unemployed by as much as three-fourths.

Finally, we have briefly considered certain implications of this study for national health insurance.

ORGANIZATION OF THE BOOK

The remainder of the book is organized as follows: Chapter 2 reviews the literature, indicates analytic issues for subsequent investigation, and discusses the desirability of extending health insurance to the unemployed. Chapter 3 reports the cross-tabular or descriptive studies. Chapter 4 reports the multivariate or behavioral studies and Chapter 5 explores the policy implications.

NOTES

1. "Health Insurance for the Unemployed," Statement by the AFL-CIO Executive Council, February 17, 1965, Bal Harbour, Florida.
2. The Social Security Amendments of 1972 extended health insurance protection under Medicare to 2 million disabled persons.
3. Although Medicaid was never intended as a program of public health insurance for the unemployed, it sometimes serves that function because in some states a person may now become eligible for Medicaid due to loss of employment.
4. Legislation requiring that employers offer continuation of group health insurance to laid-off workers has been enacted in Rhode Island.

2

Loss of Health Insurance by the Unemployed as an Analytic Interest

INTRODUCTION

In this chapter we consider the relevant questions to be asked in analyzing health insurance loss as a result of unemployment. Economists often find it useful to divide analytic questions into two categories: normative and positive. Normative questions concern "what should be," whereas positive questions concern "what is." In the context of this study the key normative question is whether the loss of health insurance by the unemployed warrants government intervention. Is it desirable that the government extend health insurance protection to the unemployed; that is, do the social and economic benefits of such a government program exceed its costs? Unfortunately, although the various considerations bearing on it can be illuminated, the present state of the art does not permit even a tentative conclusion to this crucial normative question. The positive questions are much more readily answered and receive the greatest attention in this study.

The positive questions concern the extent, kind, and distribution of health insurance lost by the unemployed; the extent to which existing public programs such as Medicaid mitigate the consequences of private health insurance loss; the behavioral determinants of health insurance loss; and the like. These questions concern what actually happens or what might happen if various emergency health insurance alternatives are enacted. How many persons would be affected? What would the cost be? The answers to these relatively simple factual questions may help to shape the answers to the more fundamental normative questions. Furthermore, if the normative question is answered in the affirmative, the factual data can facilitate the design and orderly introduction of an appropriate policy response.

THE NORMATIVE QUESTION:
SHOULD THE GOVERNMENT PROVIDE
HEALTH INSURANCE FOR THE UNEMPLOYED?

Congress's interest in the loss of health insurance by the unemployed may signal existence of a problem; unemployed persons who have lost their health insurance surely perceive it as being a problem. However it is not clear, a priori, that health insurance loss is any more or less important than various other societal and personal problems. In particular, given the reality of scarce social and economic resources, is it efficient for society to allocate some of those resources toward maintaining the health insurance of the unemployed? Why should health insurance be singled out for special attention?[1] Caspar W. Weinberger, former Secretary of Health, Education and Welfare, has argued that it is inappropriate to emphasize health insurance at the expense of more general needs that the unemployed have:

> *While many things have been done and can be done to help alleviate the economic condition of the unemployment, I would suggest that building an "in kind" benefits program is not a constructive step.*
>
> *In addition to the proposals we are discussing today [several of the bills to extend "emergency" health insurance to the unemployed], there is currently before Congress a proposal that would pay home mortgage payments during periods of unemployment, or if income is otherwise substantially reduced. What about utility bills and car payments? How far do we go in providing new "in kind" benefit programs?*
>
> *The main problem of the unemployed is not lack of health insurance. The major problem for the unemployed is that they have lost their jobs. And the most important thing we can do for them is to improve the economic situation so they can get them back. The unemployed need money—money to provide for their basic needs until they do become reemployed—money until they are able to pro-*

vide for themselves through their own employment. (Health Insurance and the Unemployed, *Hearings Before the Committee on Finance, U.S. Senate, p. 35.)*

We now attempt to respond to this kind of concern. In particular, we indicate several market problems that may justify an "in kind" program of health insurance benefits for the unemployed.

Much of the health economics literature (for example, Phelps 1973, Feldstein 1975) tends to assume, despite evidence to the contrary, that the market for health care services approximates the textbook model of perfect competition such that uninsured demands for health care correctly reflect the optimal level of health care utilization.[2] Health insurance—especially publicly subsidized health insurance—is consequently viewed as distorting the "true" demands and leading to inefficient allocation or misallocation of health care resources.

It is well known that health insurance, public or private, entails a "moral hazard" in the sense that it reduces the perceived price of health care below its actual marginal cost, creating a bias toward inefficient overutilization of health services. The recurrent finding that persons with health insurance have larger health care expenditures than those without is often put forth as evidence of this effect. (We shall in Chapter 4 suggest a different interpretation of that finding.) Furthermore, the general cost pass-through nature of insurance reimbursement is thought to inhibit price competition and lead to excess profits as providers, especially physicians, raise fees without fear of reducing demand. More recently, policy analysts have been concerned that health insurance is also an impetus to inefficiency in production of services—for example, underutilization of facilities, excess staffing, and unnecessary investment in capital equipment.

Though these arguments have merit, we are concerned that such "cost control" considerations have dominated the discussion of public health insurance (that is, Medicare and Medicaid) at the expense of another efficiency consideration. There has been a tendency to view the ongoing national health insurance debate as an equity-efficiency quandary in the sense that national health insurance results in less efficiency but greater "equity." (Recall that efficiency refers to the allocation of scarce resources in such a way as to maximize output of goods and services and that equity refers to the normatively desired distribution of these goods and services.) We believe that this may not be the most relevant dichotomization of the issue and that it is potentially damaging inasmuch as it diverts attention from a more fundamental trade-off: cost control versus efficient investment in human resources. "Health" is a human capital kind of resource in the sense that it increases one's productive capacity, as proxied by present and future earnings. An early study (Rice 1966) showed that $23.8 billion was lost to the economy in 1963 because of work-days lost due to pre-retirement death, illness, and disability. More recent studies (such as Luft 1973) suggest that "ill health" also depresses the productivity, as proxied by wages, of those still working. Health care expenditure is thus an investment in human capital to the extent that it restores or maintains the productive capacity associated with good health. However, health care expenditure may also be viewed as an investment in nonmarket- or nonearnings-related human resources to the extent that it enhances health status and thereby alleviates the future pain, discomfort, or embarrassment associated with continuing ill health and that detract from the "quality of life"—social welfare more broadly defined than the components included in the Gross National Product.

The advocates of national health insurance insist that a more comprehensive public health insurance program would promote a more equal distribution of health care services and would be more consistent with the distribution of health care "needs." Though this may reflect a concern for income distributional equity, it may also reflect a concern for efficient investment in both market and nonmarket human resources. Ignorance of the benefits from health care, uncertainty about the effectiveness of treatment in any given case, or shortage of financial assets coupled with inability to borrow against future earnings, may lead to underinvestment in health for some persons. Because more comprehensive public health insurance, including health insurance for the unemployed, would "distort" toward greater investment in health-type human resources, it would mitigate the severity of any such market failure.

Unfortunately, we do not presently know whether underinvestment in health care is a problem. Though health insurance has been shown to increase health care expenditures, it is not clear whether the additional health care expenditure improves health status and enhances productive capacity or future well-being more broadly defined.

In *Who Shall Live,* (1974) Victor R. Fuchs contends—as have others[3]—that health care is no longer a major determinant of health status in the United States, that health status is more importantly related to such life-style characteristics as diet, exercise, smoking, drinking, and work behavior. Though this thesis is compelling, even on the basis of the rather casual evidence presented, it does not preclude the possibility that the "marginal" benefits (broadly defined) of health care exceed the "marginal" costs, even if the net "marginal" contribution to health status is "small" in an absolute sense. Nor does this thesis preclude the possibility that targeted health care interventions may be efficient—that is, that benefits exceed the costs for at least some identifiable segments of the population even if not for the average employed individual. Unfortunately, the evidence for the marginal benefits thesis is as casual as the evidence that life-style is more important than health care. For example, Karen Davis (1976) finds that low-income persons have shown considerable improvement in health status over the ten-year interval since the advent of Medicaid. Infant mortality declined by 33 percent; the age-adjusted death rate declined by 10 percent; deaths from heart disease declined by 16 percent; deaths from cerebrovascular disease declined by 18 percent; and deaths from diabetes mellitus declined by 7 percent. Although it is not possible to causally attribute this improvement in the health of low-income families to Medicaid alone, given that a multitude of other factors also changed over the ten-year interval, the finding is at least consistent with that hypothesis.

More important to this study, research to date has shown a broad inverse relationship between adverse economic changes and health status. In particular, the prevalence of suicide, mental hospitalization, cirrhosis mortality, cardiovascular and renal disease, and infant, fetal, and maternal mortality have been shown to vary substantially with the rate of unemployment (see Harvey Brenner). That is, the social and economic stress associated with unemployment has been shown to damage health status and lead to longer-term and permanent reductions in both the productive capacity of our economy and in other factors affecting the quality of life. Furthermore, this increase in morbidity is coupled with a decline in the use of health services caused by the decreased purchasing power of the unemployed and by their loss of health insurance. We do not know, however, whether a greater level of health care for the unemployed can mitigate the health and human resource consequences of unemployment.

We believe that a broad program of new research is needed to answer such questions reliably—to decide whether marginal health care investments are efficient, either for the population at large or for such specific subgroups as the low-income or the unemployed. This is possibly the most important issue in health services research today and has the greatest consequence for the future of public involvement in the health care sector.

Of course, because such an ambitious research agenda cannot be covered in a single study, we cannot deal analytically with this "efficiency" question—that is, we cannot answer whether it is desirable for the government to extend health insurance protection to the unemployed to promote more efficient investment in human resources. However, public financing of health insurance for the unemployed may be socially efficient even if significant health benefits cannot be shown—that is, the existence of such benefits is a sufficient condition but not a necessary one. Consider the following alternatives that may also warrant government intervention.

First, emergency health insurance for the unemployed may be viewed, despite disclaimers to the contrary, as a stepping-stone to national health insurance. More comprehensive public health insurance, including the expansion of public health insurance to the unemployed, necessarily brings us nearer to national health insurance. If it is true, as alleged, that there are economies of scale and other efficiencies that would accrue to national health insurance—such as savings in marketing and administration, and benefits from more centralized cost control—we might see any movement toward national health insurance as being efficient in the long run, even if it is not efficient in the short run. The allegations of benefits from national health insurance are largely unsubstantiated and can be countered by opposing allegations that national health insurance would be inefficient, resulting in overinsurance for some persons and reducing the willingness to avoid injury and illness. Whether or not the benefits of national health insurance exceed its costs is not easy to determine. Nevertheless, we wish to acknowledge the relationship between the larger issue and the more specific one with which we are concerned.

Second, income distributional equity may also be a relevant factor. As Secretary Weinberger asserted, a major problem of the unemployed is lack of money. The state and federal governments have responded to this problem by providing cash benefits through unemployment compensation and related programs—presumably for income-distributional equity reasons. However, many persons contend that the present level of benefits is too low. If that is true, an increase in cash benefits would be the preferred or most efficient alternative for satisfying the income distribution norm. However, in the event that an increase in cash benefits is not politically feasible, an in-kind program of benefits such as health insurance for the unemployed may be a second-best alternative. Unfortunately, we cannot assess the importance of this prospect because there is no consensus on what is demanded by the income-distributional equity norm. In general, standards of equity are either ambiguous or nonexistent. We can only hope that whatever emerges from the political process will satisfy the equity imperatives of our society.

Finally, as we suggest in Chapter 4, much of the reduction in health insurance due to unemployment reflects shortcomings in the predominant work-group institutional mechanism for financing health insurance in this country. The economies of scale (and substantially lower price) associated with "group" or collective procurement of health insurance imply that health insurance is a collective-consumption good and therefore that the private market may not provide it in efficient quantities. Though the workplace provides a private market setting in which the pecuniary externality is internalized for most workers, no comparable mechanism for internalizing the externality is presently available to the unemployed. The market fails to provide an institutional alternative for that purpose (a thesis developed more fully in Chapter 5). If such a market failure exists, public intervention of some kind is warranted. However, as we suggest in Chapter 5, actual public provision of health insurance to the unemployed may not be the most appropriate alternative.

POSITIVE ISSUES: A REVIEW
OF WHAT IS KNOWN ABOUT THE LOSS
OF HEALTH INSURANCE BY THE UNEMPLOYED

To respond appropriately to the loss of health insurance by the unemployed, we must also have answers to certain positive or descriptive questions. For example: (1) What is the extent, kind, and distribution of health insurance lost by the unemployed? (2) How well does Medicaid substitute for loss of private health insurance? (3) What are the behavioral determinants and consequences of health insurance loss? The answers to such questions may be expected to influence the form and substance of any response to the alleged problem. In this section we review what is known about the answers to these positive questions so that we may identify those questions which remain unanswered or which have not been answered reliably from existing sources. The resultant list of unanswered and imperfectly answered questions becomes the primary agenda for this study.

We begin with some background information on health care expenditure and health insurance in the United States. Total health care expenditures in 1976 are estimated to have been $139.3 billion, equal to $638 per capita. The personal health component is $120.4 billion, or $551 per capita. Direct, out-of-pocket payments accounted for 33.5 percent of this amount; private health insurance paid 26 percent; the government (through such programs as Medicare and Medicaid) paid 40 percent; and philanthropy and industry accounted for 1 percent of such personal health expenditures. Consumer payments—defined as out-of-pocket payments plus private health insurance payments—amounted to $70 billion, which is $323 per capita, and private health insurance paid 45 percent of this amount, equal to $31 billion in total and $144 per capita.[4] Private health insurance paid 80 percent of consumer payments for hospital care, 48 percent of consumer payments for physicians' services, 14 percent of consumer payments for dentists' services, 7 percent of consumer payments for drugs and drug sundries, and 7 percent of payments for all other services. The financing of personal health care expenditures by type of expenditure is shown in Table 2-1.

Marjorie S. Mueller (1976) estimates that in 1973 approximately 78 percent of the civilian population under age 65 were covered by private health insurance for hospital and surgical care.[5] Lesser fractions of the population were covered for other health care costs—35 percent for physician visits, 11 percent for dental care, 65 percent for prescribed drugs, 62 percent for private duty nursing, 63 percent for visiting nurse services, and 33 percent for nursing home costs.

Mueller further estimates that 41 million Americans under 65 did not have private health insurance in 1973. However, many of these persons received assistance with health care costs through public programs such as Medicaid, the civilian health and medical programs for uniformed services (CHAMPUS), the Veterans Administration programs, state disability insurance programs, and workmen's compensation. In 1973 Medicaid payments were made on behalf of an estimated 20.9 million persons. These were primarily the categorical poor, including children (45.2 percent) and persons aged 65 and over (16.8 percent). Many Medicaid recipients, however, also had private health insurance, and because of the overlap in private and public health insurance coverage,

Table 2-1 Amount and Percentage Distribution of Personal Health Care Expenditures Paid by Third Parties, by Type of Expenditure, 1974

Type of Expenditure	Total	Direct Payments	Third-Party Payments			
			Total	Private Health Insurance	Government	Philanthropy and Industry
Aggregate Amount (in millions)						
Total	$120,431	$39,099	$81,332	$31,359	$48,417	$1,556
Hospital care	55,400	4,909	50,491	19,443	30,396	652
Physicians' services	26,350	10,198	16,152	9,502	6,632	18
Dentists' services	8,600	6,970	1,630	1,160	469	—
Drug and drug sundries	11,168	9,423	1,745	721	1,023	—
All other services	18,913	7,598	11,315	533	9,896	886
Per Capita Amount						
Total	$551.50	$179.05	$372.46	$143.61	$221.72	$7.13
Hospital care	253.70	22.48	231.22	89.04	139.20	2.98
Physicians' services	120.67	46.70	73.97	43.51	30.37	.08
Dentists' services	39.38	31.92	7.46	5.31	2.15	—
Drugs and drug sundries	51.14	43.15	7.99	3.30	4.69	—
All other services	86.61	34.79	51.81	2.44	45.32	4.06
Percentage Distribution						
Total	100.0	32.5	67.5	26.0	40.2	1.3
Hospital care	100.0	8.9	91.1	35.1	54.9	1.2
Physicians' services	100.0	38.7	61.3	36.1	25.2	a
Dentists' services	100.0	81.0	19.0	13.5	5.5	—
Drugs and drug sundries	100.0	84.4	15.6	6.5	9.2	—
All other services	100.0	40.2	59.8	2.9	52.3	4.7

Source: Robert M. Gibson and Marjorie Smith Mueller, "National Health Expenditures, Fiscal Year 1976," *Social Security Bulletin* (April 1977), table 3.

aLess than 1 percent.

the percentage of persons having no insurance-type assistance with health care costs is unknown.

The extent and kind of employment-related group health insurance suggests the extent and kind of health insurance that is lost by the unemployed. Walter W. Kolodrubetz (1974) has investigated the structure of such health insurance among full-time employees:

1. In 1972 an estimated 46 million full-time workers—7 out of 10— were covered by group health insurance plans on their jobs.

2. Almost half of all workers in group insurance plans had hospital, surgical, and major medical coverage. Most of the remainder had both hospital and surgical coverage.

3. About a third of the workers in group health insurance plans were in noncontributory plans with the employer paying the full cost. The employer paid at least part of the premium cost for another 47 percent of the workers.

For a variety of reasons, however, the extent and kind of group health insurance among the employed may not reflect the extent and kind of health insurance lost due to unemployment. In particular, group health insurance may be converted to an individual insurance plan or may be continued into the layoff or unemployment period. The Bureau of Labor Statistics sampled plans filed with the Department of Labor under the Welfare and Pension Plan Disclosure Act and found that two-fifths of the workers with employment-related health insurance had coverage that extended for at least a month during layoffs. Furthermore, almost half the plans that provided for continuation maintained the benefits for three months or longer. About three-fifths of plans with continuation provisions involved no change in financing. (See Table 2-2 for further results.) Kolodrubetz has independently estimated from 1972 data that about 40 percent of workers with employment-related group health insurance have benefits that extend one or more months; that 25 percent have benefits that extend three or more months; that 15 percent have benefits that extend five or more months; and that 7 percent have benefits that extend twelve or more months.

Although one can make inferences about the structure of health insurance among the unemployed from this kind of information, such indirect estimation can neglect important elements of the behavioral relationship between national economic conditions and the structure of health insurance. Reliable analysis therefore depends on a more direct inquiry into the structure of health insurance among the unemployed.

Table 2-2   Significant Characteristics of Layoff Continuation Provisions in Employee Health Plans

Health Plan Characteristics		Percentage of Workers
Total health plans studied		100.0
With specific layoff continuation provision		40.1
Without specific layoff continuation provision		59.9
Total health plans with layoff continuation period		100.0
Duration of layoff continuation period		
1 but less than 3 months		18.4
3 months or longer		47.4
Other		34.2
Effect of layoff on method of financing		
No immediate effect		78.1
No change in method of financing	63.2	
Delayed change in method of financing	14.9	
Immediate effect		21.9
Health plans with solely employer-financed benefits for active workers		100.0
With layoff continuation provision		45.0
Without layoff continuation provision		55.0
Health plans with jointly financed benefits for active workers		100.0
With layoff continuation provision		22.0
Without layoff continuation provision		78.0

Source: Bureau of Labor Statistics

Only Charles E. Phelps (1973) has done this. He analyzed 1970 data and found that only 27 percent of persons in families with an unemployed head have health insurance, compared to 88 percent for persons in families with a full-time employed head.[6] (See Table 2–3.) These results might be used to estimate that 61 percent (88 percent minus 27 percent) of unemployed workers lost their health insurance as a result of unemployment.

Estimating the impact of unemployment on the extent and kind of health insurance by simply comparing coverage of employed and unemployed workers, however, may be misleading. Those workers who tend to become unemployed may not be as likely to have group health insurance as is the typical or "average" employed worker. Thus, if the loss of health insurance caused by unemployment were estimated by taking the difference between employed and unemployed health insurance enroll-

Table 2-3   Private Health Insurance Enrollment Rates in 1970 (percentages)

Labor Force Status of Family Head	All Incomes	Poor (under $3,000)	Near poor ($3,000 to $5,000)	Middle Income ($7,000 to $10,000)	High Income (over $15,000)
Full-time employed	88	41	73	89	98
Part-time employed	44	35	52	62	—
Disabled[a]	38	20	41	—	—
Unemployed	27	4	20	—	—
All families in income class	76	38	65	92	95

Source: Charles E. Phelps, "Testimony Before U.S. House of Representatives, Subcommittee on Public Health and Environment" (Santa Monica: The Rand Corporation, December 14, 1973).

[a]Many of these persons are now covered under Medicare.

ment rates, we might overestimate the true magnitude of the loss. To obtain more reliable estimates we must also compare the health insurance of the unemployed to the health insurance of those employed workers at-risk of becoming unemployed. Alternatively, multivariate procedures may be used to control for any differences between the employed and unemployed populations.

These findings are quite limited and we see that very little is reliably known about the loss of health insurance by the unemployed. Indeed, except for the simple enrollment rate, we know virtually nothing about the health insurance that the unemployed have. Thus, a number of important questions remain to be answered in this book:

> How do the benefits compare? How "bad" or how "good" is the coverage lost due to unemployment?

> What about overlapping coverages? Do laid-off workers who have lost their group health insurance have alternative sources, either group insurance from a working spouse or individually purchased (nongroup) health insurance?

> How is the loss of health insurance by the unemployed distributed among the various SES and industry-occupation groups?

> How well do existing governmental programs such as Medicaid compensate for the loss of private health insurance?

NOTES

1. Health insurance might merely seem to be different from other goods and services because with the predominant fringe benefit of employer contribution toward financing of health insurance the workers appear to be losing a "costless" benefit.

2. See Kenneth J. Arrow (1963) for a discusison of "market failure" in the medical care and health insurance markets.

3. For example, see Richard Auster et al. (1969).

4. For most persons these per capita amounts underestimate the true financial burden because Medicare and Medicaid recipients, who have small consumer payments, are also included.

5. Nearly everyone over age 65 is now covered by Medicare.

6. In Chapter 3 we tabulate health insurance from this same source and find that 33 percent of the unemployed had health insurance. It is possible that Phelps (1973) did not reweight the data to make it nationally representative. Because low-income persons were oversampled in the survey, unweighted tabulation might be expected to give a lower estimate.

3

Health Insurance Loss Due to Unemployment— A Cross-Tabular Investigation

INTRODUCTION

In this chapter, we use cross-tabular procedures to investigate the impact of unemployment on the demand for and access to health insurance. In Chapter 4, we will use multivariate procedures for the same broad purpose. Though this chapter gives a more descriptive appraisal of the problem—that is, the extent, kind, and distribution of health insurance lost—Chapter 4 is more analytic—that is, it provides an understanding of the underlying behavioral or causal factors. Both have important implications for the development of public policy in this area, but because they answer fundamentally different questions they should not be viewed as substitutes for each other but rather as complements.

In this chapter, we first examine the extent and kind of private health insurance lost due to unemployment; next we consider the distribution of such health insurance loss; and finally we investigate the extent to which existing public programs such as Medicaid mitigate the consequences of private health insurance loss.

THE EXTENT AND KIND OF PRIVATE HEALTH INSURANCE LOST DUE TO UNEMPLOYMENT

In this section we tabulate private health insurance coverage parameters—such as covered services, deductibles, and maximum payments as well as the simple existence of health insurance—by employment status (employed or unemployed) to make inferences about the extent and kind of health insurance lost due to unemployment.[1] Health insurance coverage will be tabulated from four different data sources, each of which is a national probability sample or can be weighted to approximate a national probability sample. Each is identified and briefly discussed next.

1. *1970 CHAS-NORC Survey of Health Services Utilization and Expenditure* (CHAS). The Center for Health Administration Studies and the National Opinion Research Center conducted this fourth in a series of comprehensive surveys on health care and health care financing. In early 1971, 3,765 families were surveyed about their health insurance coverage, health care utilization, and health care expenditures in 1970. To the extent possible those data were verified by contacting the respondents' physicians, hospitals, and insurance companies. Unfortunately, persons unemployed at the end of 1970 could not be identified from CHAS unless they also had been unemployed at the time of the survey, one to three months later.[2] Thus workers with shorter periods of unemployment are not included in the CHAS sample of unemployed, making it more nearly representative of the hard-core unemployed.

2. *April 1972 Survey of Pension Plans and Health Insurance* (PPHI). PPHI is a special supplement to the April 1972 Current Population Survey (CPS) and was conducted in half the CPS sample households. For each family member 16 years of age or older who ever held a full-time job, PPHI asked about pension plans and group health insurance from the most recent employer. (It did not obtain information on individual health insurance, however.) Approximately 25,000 such records were merged with records from the April 1972 CPS.

3. *1974 Health Interview Survey* (HIS). The Health Interview Survey is an annual survey of health care conducted by the National Center for Health Statistics. The 1974 HIS was administered to 37,000 households and included questions on health insurance.

4. *1975-76 CHAS-NORC Medical Access Study* (MAS). This survey, conducted in late 1975 and early 1976 by the Center for Health Administration Studies and the National Opinion Research Center, questioned 7,500 individuals about their access to health care, including health insurance coverage.

Tabulating the health insurance characteristics from multiple data sources—CHAS, PPHI, HIS, and MAS—should provide a useful cross-check on the validity of findings from any single data source, especially because much of the information is self-reported. Although the 1970 CHAS may seem dated, it is important to examine it because its data are substantially verified and thus are thought to have greater validity. Furthermore, CHAS obtained more detailed information—such as the amount of premium, deductible, maximum payment, and coinsurance— than the other surveys.

Health insurance coverages are tabulated here by household because principal health insurance coverage is almost always purchased collectively by a family or household; that is, the household is the relevant economic unit.[3] Furthermore, we use coverage of the household head as a proxy for coverage of the entire family.[4] Although a working spouse may have health insurance while the head does not, or the head may have health insurance while other family members do not, these circumstances generally have little empirical importance.[5] In any event, these second-order effects are ignored here.

The extent of health insurance lost can be simply (but crudely) estimated from the difference between employed and unemployed coverage. If x percent of employed persons are found to have health insurance and y percent of unemployed persons have it, the number of people who have lost health insurance due to unemployment could be estimated as

$$N_u^* \, (x-y)$$

where N_u is the number of unemployed persons. However, this procedure may be inappropriate for the following reason. To the extent that employed persons who tend to become unemployed are systematically different from other employed persons and have systematically different demands for and access to health insurance, the simple calculation suggested above yields a biased estimate of the health insurance loss.[6] In fact, as we will see, the probability of having had health insurance while employed varies inversely with the expectation of unemployment, which in turn implies that the above calculation overestimates the health insurance loss.

Because of this problem, it is also important to examine the health insurance coverages of those employed persons with a greater than average expectation of unemployment—those at-risk of unemployment. If z percent of such at-risk employed workers have health insurance, it may be that the loss of health insurance due to unemployment can be estimated more reliably as $N_u^* \, (z-y)$. However, this statistic may understate the health insurance loss because even those employed persons having a small (but not zero) expectation of becoming unemployed—and who are thus excluded from the at-risk group—nevertheless become unemployed on occasion. Because such persons are more likely to have health insurance, the probability of having had health insurance while employed is underestimated from the coverage of at-risk workers only.

For these reasons, we have tabulated the health insurance coverages from the various data sources for (1) all employed heads, (2) the at-risk employed, and (3) the unemployed.[7] The at-risk workers were identified as follows. In Appendix A, "Modeling the Incidence of Unemployment Among Household Heads," we estimate a twin linear probability function that models the annual duration, in weeks, of unemployment. We then used this model to estimate the expected annual duration of unemployment for workers actually employed at the time of survey.[8] Workers were included in the at-risk sample if their predicted duration of unemployment exceeded the mean duration of unemployment, equal to 1.56 weeks, for all household heads in the 1975 Current Population Survey. We thus identified approximately 30 to 35 percent of employed workers from the various data sources as being at-risk, when the data were weighted to be nationally representative.[9]

The tabulation results are shown in Table 3-1. Our findings uniformly support the underlying hypothesis that the loss of health insurance due to unemployment is substantial. All four data sources indicate that the unemployed have much lower levels of health insurance than do either the employed or the at-risk unemployed subgroup.

1. The 1970 CHAS found that 33 percent of the unemployed have private health insurance, compared to 86 percent and 73 percent, respectively, for the employed and at-risk workers.

2. The 1972 PPHI found that 27 percent of the unemployed have group health insurance, compared to 73 percent and 60 percent, respectively, for the employed and at-risk groups. These figures are not fully comparable to those above because CHAS includes persons with individual private health insurance, but PPHI does not.

3. The 1974 HIS found that 60 percent of the unemployed have hospital insurance, compared to 88 percent and 80 percent, respectively, for the employed and at risk groups. (Almost all health insurance policies include hospital coverage.)

4. The 1975-76 MAS found that 54 percent of the unemployed have health insurance, compared to 89 percent and 82 percent, respectively, for the employed and the at-risk. The difference between HIS and MAS estimates of the health insurance coverage rate for the unemployed is not statistically significant. All else equal, HIS could be expected to yield the

Table 3-1 Health Insurance Coverage, by Employment Status of Household Head, Various Years

Health Insurance Coverage, by Data Source	Employment Status		
		At-Risk	
	Employed	Employed	Unemployed
CHAS (1970)			
Any health insurance	86.3% (1,413)	73.4% (883)	33.3% (159)
Group	75.7% (1,413)	64.1% (883)	23.6% (159)
Individual	15.2% (1,413)	13.5% (883)	10.4% (159)
Surgical	84.7% (1,413)	71.7% (883)	32.6% (159)
Hospital	86.3% (1,413)	73.4% (883)	33.4% (159)
Maximum per day	$28.6 (293)	$27.9 (183)	$27.6 (14)
Number of days covered	172.7 (732)	158.8 (373)	169.7 (23)
Percent of reasonable and customary charges	96.8% (164)	96.9 (67)	98.3% (6)
Doctor visit	63.5% (1,413)	50.7 (883)	22.4% (159)
Major medical	54.8% (1,413)	43.3% (883)	18.6% (159)
Deductible	$104 (471)	$97 (225)	$115 (10)
Co-insurance	20.3% (464)	20.4% (228)	20.0% (10)
Maximum payment	$21,250 (482)	$19,208 (233)	$24,318 (11)
Drug	55.3% (1,413)	43.9% (883)	18.8% (159)
Dental	12.8% (1,413)	10.4% (883)	3.3% (159)
Total amount of premium	$317 (603)	$258 (284)	$280 (19)
Amount of premium paid by individual	$207 (603)	$170 (284)	$258 (19)
PPHI (1972)[a]			
Group	73.4% (11,071)	60.4% (159)	26.9% (368)
Hospital	72.2% (11,071)	57.2% (159)	26.4% (368)
Surgical	71.5% (11,071)	56.6% (159)	26.6% (368)
Physician visits	34.3% (11,071)	25.2% (159)	10.5% (368)
HIS (1974)			
Hospital	88.4% (17,687)	79.8% (811)	59.6% (827)
Surgical	86.4% (17,687)	76.6% (811)	58.4% (824)
MAS (1975–76)			
Any health insurance	88.9% (2,263)	82.5% (970)	53.9% (146)
Group	81.5% (2,263)	74.7% (970)	38.0% (146)
Individual	13.2% (2,263)	15.8% (970)	19.1% (146)
Hospital	88.6% (2,253)	81.8% (968)	53.5% (144)
Surgical	88.2% (2,247)	81.7% (961)	53.5% (144)
Drugs	37.3% (2,066)	30.8% (903)	19.2% (139)
Dental	21.8% (2,172)	21.3% (940)	15.8% (144)
Doctor visits	50.0% (2,175)	45.0% (931)	30.9% (141)
Pays all	7.6% (2,175)	10.5% (931)	3.8% (141)
Major Medical	74.7% (2,045)	64.1% (860)	39.0% (134)

Source: Tabulated from indicated data sources. Sample size shown in parentheses.

[a]Employment-related group health insurance only.

more reliable estimate because of its much larger sample size. Of course, the somewhat reduced coverage rate estimated from MAS may also reflect deepening of the recession in 1976.

The values for the at-risk workers invariably fall between those for the employed and those for the unemployed—that is, persons most likely to become unemployed are also less likely to have had health insurance while employed. This suggests that we can obtain a lower-bound estimate for the probability of losing health insurance due to unemployment by taking the difference between the at-risk (z) and unemployed (y) health insurance coverage rates ($z - y$), and an upper-bound estimate by taking the difference between the employed (x) and the unemployed (y) health insurance coverage rates ($x - y$). These estimates are shown in Table 3-2. (The PPHI estimates here are more directly comparable to the others because the prevalence of individual health insurance is not so much changed by loss of employment.)

The most recent 1975–76 MAS estimates indicate that between 29 and 35 percent of the unemployed have lost health insurance due to the loss of employment. The 1974 HIS gives somewhat reduced upper- and lower-bound estimates. However, the earlier 1970 CHAS and the 1972 PPHI surveys yield substantially higher estimates, reflecting lower levels of health insurance among the unemployed in those years. Furthermore, the 1970 CHAS gives somewhat higher estimates than the 1972 PPHI. Apparently, the demand for and access to health insurance by the unemployed have increased sharply during the early 1970s, thus reducing the probability of health insurance loss due to unemployment.[10] In fact, both upper- and lower-bound estimates suggest that the probability of health insurance loss has declined by at least a third from 1970 to 1975–76. Despite this, our estimates in Table 3-2 of the *number* of households losing health insurance due to unemployment suggest that more households lost health insurance in recession year 1975 than at any other time indicated. It is estimated that between 875,000 and 1,071,000 households lacked health insurance in that year because of the head's unemployment. Of course, even more would have lost their health insurance if the same number had been unemployed in 1970.

The evidence from Table 3-1 on another analytic issue is conflicting. The most recent data source, the 1975–76 MAS, indicates that the unemployed have somewhat more individual or nongroup health insurance than either employed group. That is, the MAS results suggest that some of the unemployed have substituted individual health insurance for group insurance that has been lost due to unemployment. However, find-

Table 3-2 Upper- and Lower-Bound Estimates of Health Insurance Loss Due to Unemployment, Various Years

Year	N_u	Upper -Bound		Lower -Bound	
		$x - y$	$N_u* (x - y)$	$z - y$	$N_u* (z - y)$
1970	1,418,000	53.0%	751,000	40.1%	569,000
1972 (group only)	1,673,000	46.9%	785,000	33.5%	560,000
1974 (hospital only)	1,731,000	28.8%	499,000	20.2%	350,000
1975–76[a]	3,061,000	35.0%	1,071,000	28.6%	875,000

Source: x, y, and z—Table 3-1; N_u—Handbook of Labor Statistics (1976), table 63, p. 132.

N_u—number of unemployed household heads.

x —percentage of employed heads with health insurance

y —percentage of unemployed heads with health insurance

z —percentage of at-risk employed heads with health insurance

[a]N_u for 1975–76 is the mean of 1974 and 1975 values.

ings from the much earlier 1970 CHAS indicate just the opposite—the unemployed have less individual health insurance. We cannot explain this discrepancy. In any event, the extent of substitution is nominal. Even if the MAS results are correct, the probability that an unemployed worker has individual health insurance is only 5.9 percentage points higher than it is for the employed at large; it is 3.3 percentage points higher than for employed workers at risk of unemployment. From these figures, we estimate that only 10 to 14 percent of workers losing group health insurance have substituted individual, nongroup health insurance. If group and nongroup insurance were equivalent in price and quality this result might be surprising. In fact, however, individual or nongroup insurance costs 70 to 80 percent more than otherwise equivalent group insurance. Furthermore, most employers pay at least part of the group health insurance premium. Thus, individual health insurance is a very expensive substitute, and its greater cost apparently exceeds the benefits of continuing health insurance during periods of unemployment. (The relationship between group and nongroup health insurance receives further attention in Chapter 4.)

So far, our discussion has been concerned with the simple existence or nonexistence of health insurance. However, as we see from Table 3-1, the comprehensiveness or "quality" of health insurance varies widely. Though nearly anyone with health insurance has hospital and surgical coverage, such coverages as major medical, doctor visits, drugs, and dental services are more limited.[11] Using the 1975–76 MAS, we have calculated the percentages of persons with health insurance who have each of these coverages, for each of the three employment status groups— employed, at-risk, and unemployed. The results in Table 3-3 indicate that the employed have a somewhat higher probability of having major medical and drug coverages than the unemployed. Also, the at-risk employed have a higher probability of having medical coverage than the unemployed. Otherwise, the coverage rates in Table 3-3 are essentially similar across employment status categories.

Table 3-3   Service Coverage of Those with Health Insurance by Employment Status of Household Head, 1975–76

| | Employment Status | | |
Service	Employed	At-Risk Employed	Unemployed
Hospital	99.7%	99.2%	99.2%
Surgical	99.2%	99.0%	99.2%
Major medical	84.0%	77.7%	72.4%
Doctor visits	56.2%	54.5%	57.3%
pays all	15.3%	23.3%	12.3%
Drugs	42.0%	37.3%	35.6%
Dental	24.5%	25.8%	29.3%

Source: Tabulated from MAS.

In addition, the basic hospital, major medical, and doctor visit coverage parameters shown in Table 3-1 are not systematically or importantly different by employment status. For example, the mean number of days of basic hospital coverage is 173 days for the employed versus 170 days for the unemployed[12]; the mean coinsurance rate is 20.3 percent for the employed versus 20.0 percent for the unemployed; and the average maximum payment from major medical is $21,000 for the employed versus $24,000 for the unemployed. The total health insurance premium amount can also be regarded as an index of health insurance "quality," inasmuch as it reflects the expected value of benefits. Although this amount is somewhat higher for the employed, $317 compared to $280, the difference is not statistically significant.[13] The difference between the at-risk group and the unemployed is also not significant. However, the larger difference in premium amount between the employed and the at-risk is significant at the .01 level. We conclude that the quality of health insurance held by the unemployed carrying health insurance is somewhat lower but not too different from that held by the employed. This further suggests that the quality of health insurance lost due to unemployment is not much different from the average.

Unemployment also has an impact on premium cost-sharing. Dividing the individual-paid amount of the premium by the total premium amount (see Table 3-1 for both), we find that the unemployed worker pays 92 percent of the premium and that the employed and at-risk workers pay 65 percent and 66 percent respectively. Not surprisingly, the unemployed have lost nearly all the employer-paid contribution to health insurance. While such persons have not actually lost health insurance, the amount of income available for other purposes has been even further reduced, beyond the loss of wages itself, to continue health insurance during unemployment.

THE DISTRIBUTION OF HEALTH INSURANCE LOSSES

The distribution of health insurance losses due to unemployment is investigated by estimating demographic-specific health insurance coverage rates for the employed and unemployed and, as before, taking the difference between them as an upper-bound estimate for the impact of unemployment. (Lower-bound estimates are not given.) In this way we determine the characteristics of those persons who are most (or least) likely to lose health insurance because of unemployment. A more analytic investigation of the relationship between sociodemographic characteristics and health insurance appears in the next chapter.

In Table 3-4 we tabulated hospital insurance coverage from the 1974 HIS by employment status (employed and unemployed only) and by demographic characteristics of the household head.[14] We report on several demographic dimensions: age, education, race, marital status, sex, number of children, health status, family income, residential location, geographic region, occupation, and industry of employment. We shall concentrate on the differences between employed and unemployed insurance rates—our upper-bound estimate of health insurance loss—but shall also give some attention to the absolute enrollment rates. A small effect on a particular demographic group, for example, may merely reflect the fact that its members did not have much health insurance while employed. In other words, it is also important to consider the relative impact.

Table 3-4 Hospital Insurance Coverage by Employment Status and Demographic Characteristics of Household Head, 1974

Hospital Insurance Coverage, By Demographic Characteristics	Employment Status		Difference (1 minus 2)
	(1) Employed	(2) Unemployed	
Age			
30 years or less	84.0% (3,795)	47.2% (301)	36.8%
31–45	89.5% (5,397)	59.7% (243)	29.8%
46–55	90.7% (3,733)	68.5% (165)	22.2%
56–65	90.3% (2,450)	78.8% (118)	11.5%
Education			
8 years or less	80.3% (1,947)	54.4% (160)	25.9%
9–12 years	88.1% (7,964)	58.5% (463)	29.6%
More than 12 years	92.5% (5,376)	66.8% (199)	25.7%
Race			
White	89.4% (14,046)	63.6% (696)	25.8%
Nonwhite	79.4% (1,329)	38.2% (131)	41.2%
Marital Status			
Not married	81.3% (3,208)	49.4% (322)	31.9%
Married	90.5% (12,167)	66.1% (505)	24.4%
Sex			
Male	89.8% (13,417)	64.2% (611)	25.6%
Female	80.4% (1,958)	46.8% (216)	33.6%
Number of children			
0	87.8% (6,168)	61.2% (312)	26.6%
1	88.7% (3,739)	67.8% (183)	20.9%
2	90.3% (3,599)	53.4% (148)	36.9%
3	90.6% (2,077)	58.8% (85)	31.8%
4	86.4% (1,033)	54.9% (51)	31.5%
5 or more	80.6% (759)	41.3% (46)	39.3%
Health status			
Excellent	90.4% (8,032)	63.7% (300)	26.7%
Good	88.1% (5,739)	58.7% (351)	29.4%
Fair	81.2% (1,382)	56.6% (129)	24.6%
Poor	73.0% (154)	48.8% (43)	24.2%
Family income			
Less than $5,000	58.6% (930)	31.0% (245)	27.6%
$5,000–9,000	83.1% (3,461)	58.0% (257)	25.1%
$10,000–15,000	93.8% (4,654)	79.4% (160)	14.4%
$16,000–25,000	96.8% (4,104)	90.8% (98)	6.0%
Over $25,000	95.7% (1,472)	96.6% (29)	−.9%

Table 3-4   (continued)

Hospital Insurance Coverage, By Demographic Characteristics	Employment Status		Difference (1 minus 2)
	(1) Employed	(2) Unemployed	
Residential location			
Central city, SMSA	87.0% (4,585)	51.7% (265)	35.3%
Noncentral city, SMSA	91.7% (6,540)	67.0% (339)	24.7%
Non-SMSA	85.4% (4,250)	57.8% (223)	27.6%
Geographic Region			
Northeast	92.9% (3,736)	62.6% (206)	30.3%
North Central	91.9% (4,513)	72.1% (244)	19.8%
South	84.7% (4,513)	52.3% (174)	32.4%
West	83.6% (2,613)	47.8% (203)	35.8%
Occupation			
Professional, technical, and kindred workers, managers, administrators	93.0% (4,856)	67.1% (143)	25.9%
Sales, clerical, and kindred workers	90.2% (2,479)	68.0% (122)	22.2%
Craftsmen, operatives, nonfarm laborers	88.2% (6,325)	61.5% (421)	26.7%
Farm-related workers	71.7% (424)	66.7% (15)	5.0%
Service workers, private household	77.3% (1,148)	33.3% (93)	44.0%
Industry			
Agriculture	71.2% (487)	62.5% (24)	8.7%
Forestry & Fisheries	80.0% (16)	33.1% (3)	46.9%
Mining	91.8% (167)	66.7% (3)	25.1%
Construction	81.0% (1,303)	60.3% (126)	20.7%
Manufacturing	95.1% (4,741)	68.4% (228)	26.7%
Transportation and public utilities	93.8% (1,373)	63.3% (49)	30.5%
Wholesale and retail trade	83.7% (2,201)	52.6% (133)	31.1%
Finance, insurance, and real estate	90.3% (794)	70.8% (24)	19.5%
Services and miscellaneous	84.6% (2,942)	51.0% (157)	33.6%
Public administration	93.2% (1,198)	68.2% (44)	25.0%

Source: Tabulated from 1974 HIS. Sample size shown in parentheses.

Recall from Table 3-1 that 88.4 percent of the employed in the 1974 HIS had hospital insurance and that 59.6 percent of the unemployed had hospital insurance. Taking the difference between these two figures, 28.8 percent is our upper-bound estimate for the average probability of losing health insurance as a result of unemployment. Table 3-4 shows that this loss is unevenly distributed across the various age categories, with a disproportionate burden being borne by the younger workers. Even though the very youngest workers, 30 years or less, have a somewhat lower probability of having health (hospital) insurance while employed, they have the greatest probability of health insurance loss—over three times as large as for the upper-age category. Our upper-bound estimate for the probability of health insurance loss is 36.8 percent for those aged 30 years or less, compared to 11.5 percent for those aged 56–65.

The estimates of health insurance loss by education level are not too dissimilar, even though the probability of having health insurance while employed increases with education. The estimates of impact are roughly the same because the probability of having health insurance while unemployed also increases with educational level, and at approximately the same rate.

The burden of health insurance loss is over 50 percent greater for nonwhites than for whites, although nonwhites also have a 10 percentage point lower probability of having health insurance while employed. Similarly, the burden of health insurance loss is somewhat greater for unmarried household heads than it is for married heads, even though unmarried heads have a lower probability of having health insurance while employed. This same pattern is borne out when sex of the household head is considered. The impact on female-headed households is greater even though they are less likely to have health insurance when employed. Thus both the relative and absolute impacts of health insurance loss due to unemployment are greater for nonwhites and for unmarried or female household heads.

The estimated probabilities of health insurance loss are lowest for persons with one or no children and highest for those with five or more children. The probability of health insurance loss in this last category is almost twice as high as for those with only a single child. Furthermore, the probability of health insurance when employed does not vary substantially with the number of children, except that it is lower for those with five or more children, so that the relative impact is generally greater for persons with more children.

The probability of health insurance loss due to unemployment does not vary markedly with self-reported health status of the household head. However, this constancy of impact conceals concurrent variation in levels of health insurance among the employed and the unemployed. Household heads with poor health are much less likely to have health insurance while both employed and unemployed. Thus, the impact on those in poor health is relatively greater.

The extent of health insurance loss due to unemployment varies most dramatically with respect to the level of family income. The probability of health insurance loss by families with incomes in excess of $25,000 is near zero. (The $-.09$ percent estimate is not significantly different from zero.) Furthermore, the probability of health insurance loss at the next lower income level, $16,000 to $25,000, is less than a fourth of what it is for the lowest income level, under $5,000. The probability is almost half as much for the $10,000–15,000 income category as for the lowest category. We also observe the now-familiar pattern that those most impacted by loss of health insurance had the least health insurance to begin with. The probability of having health insurance while employed is less than two-thirds as much at the lowest level as it is at the higher income levels.

Looking at residential location, the probability of health insurance loss is largest for those with SMSA–central residence and is essentially similar for those with SMSA–noncentral city and non–SMSA residence. However, the probabilities of having health insurance both while employed and while unemployed are higher in SMSA–noncentral city residence.

In considering regional differences, the probability of health insurance loss is about the same in the Northeast, South, and West regions but is 10 percentage points lower in the North Central region. (We have no explanation for this finding.) Furthermore, the probability of having health insurance while employed is almost 10 percentage points higher in the Northeast and North Central regions than it is in the South and West.

Turning to occupation, service workers are the most impacted by the loss of health insurance and farm workers are the least affected. This latter result no doubt reflects, at least in part, the greater prevalence of individually purchased health insurance in farm employments. However, farm workers also have the lowest probability of having health insurance when employed. The probability is also relatively low for service workers.

The industry tabulations in Table 3–4 show that workers in agriculture, finance, insurance and real estate, and construction have the lowest probability of health insurance loss and that workers in forestry and fisheries have the highest probability of health insurance loss. The probability of having health insurance when employed is lowest for workers in agriculture, forestries and fisheries, construction, and the services and miscellaneous categories.

Table 3–5 is a tabulation of hospital and surgical coverages for both the household head and spouse by employment status of both. Once again, we use the difference between employed and unemployed coverage rates as an upper-bound estimate of the probability that health insurance is lost due to unemployment. Giving primary attention to the hospital results, we see that the probability of health insurance loss by the head is about seven percentage points lower if the head's spouse is working, presumably because the spouse has access to group health insurance from the spouse's employer. The impact on spouses' coverage is reduced even more than the impact on the head—about 12 percentage points—if the spouse is working. Except for coverage of working spouses when the head is unemployed, the head and spouse coverage rates differ by no more than a percentage point. However, a working spouse in a house-

Table 3-5 Health Insurance Coverage, by Employment Status of Both Household Head and Spouse, 1974

Health Insurance Coverage by Employment Status of Spouse	Employment Status of Head		Difference (1 minus 2)
	(1) Employed	(2) Unemployed	
Spouse not working:	Head Coverage		
Hospital	89.3% (7,319)	63.9% (299)	25.4%
Surgical	87.3% (7,319)	63.4% (298)	23.9%
Spouse working:			
Hospital	92.4% (6,269)	73.9% (184)	18.5%
Surgical	91.0% (6,269)	72.8% (184)	18.2%
Spouse not working:	Spouse Coverage		
Hospital	89.1% (7,262)	62.6% (297)	26.5%
Surgical	86.5% (7,262)	62.3% (297)	24.2%
Spouse working:			
Hospital	93.0% (6,227)	79.1% (182)	13.9%
Surgical	91.9% (6,227)	78.6% (182)	13.3%

Source: Tabulated from 1974 HIS. Sample size shown in parentheses.

hold with an unemployed head has about a six percentage point greater probability than does the head of being covered by health insurance.

Hospital and surgical coverages by employment status and sex of unmarried heads are tabulated in Table 3-6. Unmarried heads have a greater probability of health insurance loss than the married heads described in Table 3-5. However, it is noteworthy that the impact on female heads who are unmarried or whose spouses are not present is only a few percentage points higher than it is for unmarried male heads.

Health insurance coverages by duration of unemployment are tabulated in Table 3-7. Because this distributional dimension was not available from HIS these results are obtained from the 1972 PPHI and thus are not entirely comparable to the findings in Tables 3-4, 3-5, and 3-6. The mean percentage of health insurance loss (upper-bound estimate) from PPHI is 46.9 percent, compared with 28.8 percent for HIS. Table 3-7 indicates that the probability of having employment-related group health insurance declines steadily with duration of unemployment and therefore that the probability of health insurance loss is greatest for those unemployed the longest, the so-called structurally unemployed.

The size of the firm affects whether a worker has health insurance while employed. Only 47.2 percent of workers in firms employing fewer than 25 persons have health insurance while employed. In firms with 25 to 99 workers, the figure jumps to 82.8 percent, and in firms with 100 or more employees, 92.9 percent of workers have health insurance while employed. This suggests that the impact of health insurance loss is potentially greater for workers in large firms than for those in small firms. Unfortunately, we do not have data on health insurance enrollment rates

Table 3-6 Health Insurance Coverage, by Employment Status and Sex of Unmarried Heads, 1974

Health Insurance Coverage by Sex	*Employment Status*		*Difference (1 minus 2)*
	(1) Employed	*(2) Unemployed*	
Unmarried male:			
Hospital	80.9% (1,594)	50.8% (128)	30.1%
Surgical	78.2% (1,594)	46.4% (127)	31.8%
Unmarried female:			
Hospital	80.3% (2,505)	46.8% (216)	33.5%
Surgical	77.2% (2,505)	46.0% (215)	31.2%

Source: Tabulated from 1974 HIS. Sample size shown in parentheses.

Table 3-7 Group Health Insurance Coverage, by Duration of Unemployment, 1972

Duration of Unemployment	Coverage
Less than 6 weeks	35.1% (128)
7–10 weeks	24.3% (37)
11–14 weeks	20.7% (29)
15–26 weeks	30.3% (76)
27–39 weeks	11.8% (34)
40 weeks or more	14.8% (27)

Source: Tabulated from PPHI. Sample size shown in parentheses.

among the unemployed by firm size, so we cannot estimate the actual impact.

In this section we have described how health insurance loss by the unemployed is distributed among the various demographic or socioeconomic groups, and we find that it has been distributed unevenly. Perhaps the most salient finding has been that the probability of health insurance loss due to unemployment declines sharply with the level of family income. We have been careful not to attribute causation on the basis of our cross-tabular findings alone, although we attempt to do this from the multivariate analyses in Chapter 4.

MEDICAID AS A PROGRAM OF PUBLIC HEALTH INSURANCE FOR THE UNEMPLOYED

In this section we investigate whether and how well Medicaid substitutes for private health insurance lost due to unemployment.[15] Although Medicaid was never intended as a program of public health insurance for the unemployed, it sometimes serves as a substitute because a person may now become eligible for Medicaid during unemployment in some states. Nearly half the states provide AFDC benefits to families in which the father (1) has been unemployed for 30 days, (2) has some previous work experience, and (3) is not receiving unemployment insurance benefits. Because all states must provide medical assistance to AFDC recipients, these families also become eligible for Medicaid. Although Medicaid may not be satisfactory as a comprehensive and equitable program of public health insurance for the unemployed, it is nevertheless important to ascertain the extent to which it mitigates the financial burden associated with loss of private health insurance. The recognition that Medicaid offers at least a partial solution to the problem, as well as an understanding of its inability to solve the entire problem, may well affect the urgency and form of public response to the "residual" problem—the loss of private health insurance by those who are neither eligible for Medicaid nor benefit from other public and charitable assistance with health care costs.

The sources of payment for family health care, including Medicaid, by employment status of household head are tabulated in Table 3-8.[16] Although payment sources are tabulated both in dollar amounts and as percentages, we focus our attention on the percentages to control for differences in the level of health care expenditure. Though health insurance does affect the level of health care expenditures, we are reluctant to make inferences about those effects from cross-tabular findings. Nevertheless, it is noteworthy that health care expenditures by the at-risk employed group are smaller than those by either the entire employed group or the unemployed.

The percentage tabulations in Table 3-8 indicate that Medicaid, welfare, and "free" care together represent an important source of health care financing among the unemployed. (We assume that this category largely reflects the Medicaid program.) This Medicaid category accounts for 32 percent of health care expenditures by the unemployed, compared to 13 percent and 10 percent, respectively, for all employed and the at-risk employed. (The differences are significant at the .10 level.) Thus, it appears that Medicaid and related sources of health care for the poor constitute a significant program of public health insurance to the unemployed and substantially mitigate the greater financial risks (over and above loss of income) occasioned by the loss of private health insurance. In fact, the results suggest that Medicaid more than makes up the shortfall in private health insurance. Private health insurance paid 23 percent of expenditures by the unemployed, compared to 33 percent and 26 percent, respectively, for all employed and the at-risk employed. Thus, private health insurance payments have declined at most by 10 percentage points during unemployment, while Medicaid payments have increased by almost 20 percentage points. Furthermore, the "other" payments category is several percentage points higher for the unemployed. Although this category, which includes V.A. hospital care, is not explicitly income- and therefore employment-conditioned, it nevertheless seems to be a partial substitute for private health insurance.

Table 3-8 Sources of Payment for Family Health Care Expenditures, by Employment Status of Household Head, 1970

Source of Payment	Employed (N = 1413)		At-Risk (= 883)		Unemployed (N = 159)	
	Amount	Percentage	Amount	Percentage	Amount	Percentage
Private health insurance	$238	33%	$126	26%	$141	23%
Medicaid, Welfare, and free care	$ 95	13%	$ 46	10%	$198	32%
Other[a]	$ 24	3%	$ 31	6%	$ 56	9%
Out-of-pocket	$356	50%	$278	58%	$220	36%
Total	$713	100%	$480	100%	$614	100%

Source: Tabulated from weighted CHAS.

[a]Armed Forces dependent, accident, or liability insurance V.A. hospital, workmen's compensation, industrial or school health service, etc.

On balance, out-of-pocket payments account for only 36 percent of health care expense among the unemployed, compared to 50 and 58 percent, respectively, for all employed and the at-risk employed, both significantly higher. That is, the effective coinsurance or out-of-pocket payment rate is lower for unemployed persons than it is for employed persons.[17] Though this finding is significant and suggests that the loss of private health insurance due to unemployment is not a serious problem, sources of payment are tabulated from CHAS, which unfortunately excludes most persons unemployed fewer than six weeks (see p. 26 this study). Because the AFDC-Unemployed Father program, and therefore Medicaid, has a 30-day eligibility requirement, Medicaid is a less perfect substitute for the shorter-duration unemployed. On the other hand, the short-term unemployed are much more likely to still have their private health insurance. Second, even though Medicaid may substitute very well for private health insurance on average, it seems likely that it will not do so in a fully equitable fashion. After all, the Medicaid program is not intended to benefit the unemployed who have lost private health insurance. Therefore, it should not be surprising that some unemployed persons benefit from Medicaid much more than others and that some do not benefit at all. To address this distributional-equity issue we have tabulated in Table 3–9 the sources of payment by poverty status (above or below the official poverty income level) and by employment status; in Table 3–10 we have tabulated payment sources by Medicaid eligibility, but for the unemployed only.

Table 3–9 shows that Medicaid benefits are in fact concentrated on the program's nominal constituency among the unemployed—those with low incomes. Medicaid paid 54 percent of health care costs for the unemployed below the poverty line but only 15 percent of costs for those above it. However, private health insurance paid 38 percent of the costs for the unemployed above the poverty line, compared to only 4 percent for those below. On balance, the effective coinsurance or out-of-pocket payment is lower for the unemployed, above or below the poverty level, than it is for the employed.

Though we are hesitant to interpret differences in total health care expenditure figures, it deserves mention that, like the at-risk employed group in Table 3–8, employed persons below the poverty level have a smaller health care expenditure than do the unemployed, above or below the poverty line, and the employed above the poverty line. This suggests that the "working poor" have even less financial assistance with health care costs than the nonworking poor. That hypothesis is further sup-

Table 3-9 Sources of Payment for Family Health Care Expenditures, by Employment Status of Household Head and Poverty Status, 1970

| Source of Payment | Employed (N=1413) | | | | Unemployed (N=159) | | | |
| | Under Poverty Line (N=248) | | Above Poverty Line (N=1165) | | Under Poverty Line (N=109) | | Above Poverty Line (N=50) | |
	Amount	Percentage	Amount	Percentage	Amount	Percentage	Amount	Percentage
Private health insurance	$ 79	22%	$249	34%	$ 22	4%	$272	38%
Medicaid, Welfare, and free care	$ 74	20%	$ 97	13%	$281	54%	$106	15%
Other[a]	$ 17	5%	$ 24	3%	$ 52	10%	$ 59	8%
Out-of-pocket	$195	54%	$367	50%	$169	32%	$276	39%
Total	$364	100%	$737	100%	$524	100%	$713	100%

Source: Tabulated from weighted CHAS.

[a]Armed Forces dependent, accident or liability insurance, V.A. hospital, workmen's compensation, industrial or school health service, etc.

Table 3-10 Sources of Payment for Family Health Care Expenditures by Medicaid-Eligibility Status, Head of Household Unemployed, 1970.

Source of Payment	Not Medicaid-Eligible (N=84)		Medicaid-Eligible (N=75)	
	Amount	Percentage	Amount	Percentage
Private health insurance	$118	27%	$184	19%
Medicaid, Welfare, and free care	$ 0	0%	$572	60%
Other[a]	$ 55	12%	$ 54	6%
Out-of-pocket	$265	60%	$135	14%
Total	$439	100%	$945	100%

Source: Tabulated from weighted CHAS.

[a]Armed Forces, dependent, accident or liability insurance, V.A. hospital, workmen's compensation, industrial or school health service, etc.

ported by the information on source of payment. The out-of-pocket payment rate is higher for poor workers than for poor nonworkers, 54 percent versus 32 percent.

Table 3-10 tabulates payment sources by Medicaid-eligibility of the unemployed. Medicaid eligibility has been proxied from receipt of Medicaid-type benefits. That is, persons reporting payment from "Medicaid, welfare, and free care" were operationally identified as eligible for Medicaid. This definition is imperfect, but we have no alternative.

The out-of-pocket payment rate is 60 percent for the unemployed who are not Medicaid-eligible. The somewhat higher private health insurance payment rate among those not eligible for Medicaid, 27 percent versus 19 percent, does not begin to offset the sharply higher Medicaid payment rate among those who are eligible, 0 percent versus 60 percent. Only about 35 percent of the unemployed in the weighted CHAS sample were "Medicaid-eligible" by our definition. Therefore we conclude that Medicaid cannot be regarded as a comprehensive program of public health insurance for the unemployed, that at least some unemployed have neither very adequate private health insurance nor access to public health insurance alternatives. Furthermore, the health care expenditure by the Medicaid-eligible unemployed is over twice as much as that for those not eligible.[18]

An independent estimate of the residual problem—the problem of persons who have no assistance with health care costs—is provided in

Table 3-11, which reports the reasons given in the 1974 Health Interview Survey (HIS) for not having private health insurance. Almost 19 percent of the unemployed without such insurance reported that they were receiving health care from Medicaid and related sources, and another 10 percent reported that they were receiving Veterans' health benefits.[19] This suggests that about 71 percent of the unemployed without private health insurance have no apparent public health insurance alternative. Most of those persons cite the expense of private health insurance as the reason for not having it. (About 83 percent of the employed without private health insurance list no public alternatives.)

Among the unemployed without private health insurance in the 1975-76 MAS, 31 percent reported being covered by Medicaid or public aid health plans. Another 18 percent reported coverage from other sources including Medicare, workmen's compensation, V.A., and "free" clinics.[20] These estimates suggest that 51 percent of the unemployed without private health insurance do not have public assistance to offset the costs of their health care. (Among the employed without private health insurance in the 1975-1976 MAS, 39 percent reported other health plans—or, conversely, 61 percent did not report alternatives.) Note that the MAS reported on a more comprehensive list of alternatives than the HIS.

SUMMARY

The leading findings from this chapter may be summarized as follows:

1. The most recent data indicate that private health insurance enrollment rates among the unemployed are 29 to 35 percentage points lower than enrollment rates among employed persons. If we divide these figures by the percentage of employed persons with health insurance, we find that 35 to 39 percent of those who had health insurance when employed lost it when they became unemployed.

2. We estimate that during the 1974-75 recession, between 875,000 and 1,071,000 households had lost health insurance at any one time due to the unemployment of the household head.

3. The level of health insurance among the unemployed has increased sharply during the 1970s.

Table 3-11 Main Reason for not Having Private Health Insurance, by Employment Status of Household Head, 1974

Reason	Employed		At-Risk		Unemployed	
	Number	Percentage	Number	Percentage	Number	Percentage
Can't obtain insurance	35	1.7%	2	1.2%	8	2.4%
Do not believe in insurance	89	4.4%	8	5.0%	12	3.6%
Dissatisfied with previous insurance	73	3.6%	4	2.5%	4	1.2%
Care through Medicare, Medicaid, or Welfare	116	5.7%	13	8.1%	62	18.7%
Healthy	251	12.4%	17	10.6%	27	8.2%
Too expensive, can't afford	884	43.8%	82	50.9%	145	43.8%
Military care or veterans' benefits	224	11.1%	14	8.7%	33	10.0%
Other	346	17.1%	21	13.0%	40	12.1%
Total	2,018	100.0%	161	100.0%	331	100.0%

Source: Tabulated from 1974 HIS.

4. No more than 10 to 14 percent of workers losing group health insurance have substituted individual nongroup health insurance.

5. The "quality" of health insurance lost by the unemployed is somewhat lower but not too much different from the average.

6. Health insurance losses are not evenly distributed across various demographic and socioeconomic groups. The probability of health insurance loss is greatest for young workers, nonwhite workers, unmarried workers, female workers, workers with large families, low-income workers, workers living in central cities, workers outside the North Central region, and workers in selected occupations and industries. The probability of health insurance loss did not vary significantly with education or health status.

7. Households in which the spouse works have a 7 percent lower probability of health insurance loss due to unemployment of the head. Dividing this figure by the percentage probability of health insurance loss in the larger population, we estimate that the probability of losing health insurance is reduced by 27 percent.

8. Not surprisingly, the probability of health insurance loss varies directly with the duration of unemployment. That is, the "structurally" unemployed are much more likely to lose health insurance.

9. Between 19 and 31 percent of the unemployed without private health insurance receive health care from Medicaid and related sources. Another 10 to 18 percent receive at least some health care from sources like V.A. and workmen's compensation. Between 51 and 71 percent of the unemployed without private health insurance have no public health insurance alternatives whatsoever.

10. The unemployed who are not eligible for Medicaid pay 60 percent of their health care costs out-of-pocket, compared to 14 percent for Medicaid-eligibles. Furthermore, the health care expenditure for the Medicaid-eligible unemployed is over twice as much as for those not eligible.

11. The low-income employed have even less health insurance protection than the unemployed, above or below the poverty level.

In Chapter 5 we shall attempt to further interpret these findings and to explore their implications for public policy. However, we first turn to the multivariate investigation of health insurance loss by the unemployed.

NOTES

1. We are not aware of any data source that has time series information on health insurance coverage—that is, both before and after loss of employment. If such information were available the loss of health insurance due to unemployment could be estimated more directly and reliably.

2. Health insurance coverages were reported for December 31, 1970, whereas employment status was reported for date of interview. Persons unemployed at time of interview and reporting some unemployment in 1970, time unknown, were assumed to have been unemployed at the end of 1970.

3. Since completing this study, Mark S. Blumberg of Kaiser Health Plan, Inc. has called my attention to the STATS (Stimulated Tax And Transfer System) taxonomy for household enumeration developed by the Social Security Administration. In essence, each STATS unit represents an individual or family combination required to file an individual income tax form and varies from the Census designation of household heads inasmuch as secondary families and adult chilren living at home are treated as separate units. Blumberg notes that the STATS scheme corresponds much better to the universe of potential health plan subscribers. On the other hand, the intensity of public concern about individuals from a family may not be as great since unemployment does not usually pose as serious a problem for adult children still living at home as it does for most household heads. In any event, we believe that the STATS taxonomy has considerable merit and recommend taking account of it in future analyses.

4. Only heads under the age of 65 were included because almost all elderly now have Medicare.

5. Table 3–5 points out one important exception. A working spouse, head unemployed, has a 6 percentage point higher probability of having health insurance than the head.

6. An alternative way of stating the problem is to say that this procedure fails to control for variation in other nonemployment-related determinants of health insurance demand. Though this chapter proposes an indirect procedure for doing this, we also do it more directly in the next chapter by estimating the health insurance demand relationships.

7. Both part-time and full-time workers were included in the "employed" groups.

8. Unfortunately, the variable indicating level of statewide unemployment benefits (UCSTATE) could not be included in the predictive equation because geographic regions were not identified with sufficient specificity from the health insurance data sources. Furthermore, other family income (OTHINC) was not available from MAS.

9. Inferences about relative population size should not be attempted from the indicated sample size figures. In the interest of economy, the data sources were sometimes randomly sampled.

10. Of course, the results may also reflect differences in the manner in which questions were asked, as well as whether the data were verified. We discount this hypothesis, however, because a consistent pattern emerges from four different data sources.

11. Doctor visit and drug coverage rates are higher in the 1970 CHAS than in the 1975-76 MAS. Although health insurance may have become less comprehensive as we have become more sensitive to the "moral hazard" problem, these findings may also reflect self-reporting bias from the unvalidated MAS.

12. Many policies did not stipulate the number of days covered. Other responses were as follows:

	Employed	At-Risk	Unemployed
Most common semiprivate	426	192	10
85% of most common semi-private	1	0	0
80% of most common semi-private	3	1	0
75% of most common semi-private	2	1	0
No maximum	3	2	0
Ward rate	15	7	0

13. We have not controlled for the relatively greater prevalence of individual insurance among the unemployed. In consequence, the magnitude of the quality difference is underestimated.

14. Almost all health insurance policies include hospital coverage.

15. Medicaid is the joint federal-state program that finances health care for many low-income persons, mostly welfare recipients.

16. The table reflects the estimated monetary value of care provided "free" or at reduced rate as well as actual expenditures.

17. The unemployed worker is further advantaged in the following sense. The actuarial value of private health insurance payments is included in the health insurance premium amount that is paid, either directly or indirectly, by the insured party. That is, the private health insurance payment is ultimately an out-of-pocket expense. On the other hand, the Medicaid program is not financed by benefit recipients; it is an income transfer program. In this sense, the out-of-pocket amount from Table 3-8 plus the private health insurance payment may give a better estimate of the actual financial burden of health care. These two sources together account for 83 percent of expenditures by the employed, 84 percent by the at-risk, and only 59 percent by

the unemployed. This suggests that the unemployed have it much easier than the employed, on average.

18. Our proxy identification of Medicaid-eligibles also biases the estimates in this direction. Persons who were in fact Medicaid-eligible but did not have any health care expenditures will not have received Medicaid benefits and thus were included in the noneligible sample. We do not believe, however, that this bias is serious.

19. This may reflect the unemployment of veterans newly returned from Vietnam.

20. Workmen's compensation cannot be regarded as being a very close substitute for private health insurance; it covers only work-related medical expense. Furthermore, like other alternatives cited, it does not extend to all members of the family.

4

The Loss of Health Insurance Due to Unemployment—A Multivariate Investigation

INTRODUCTION

Cross-tabular or descriptive analyses were used in Chapter 3 to investigate the impact of unemployment on the demand for and access to health insurance. Though such an analysis is useful and answers many policy-relevant questions about the loss of health insurance by the unemployed, the cross-tabular approach also has important limitations and is not adequate for answering some questions. In particular, cross-tabular procedures cannot be used to isolate the underlying determinants of health insurance loss. Multivariate procedures, which are more appropriate for this purpose, are used here to analyze the loss of health insurance caused by unemployment and to isolate those factors that, in addition to employment itself, influence the magnitude of insurance coverage. As we shall see in Chapter 5, the causal mechanism has important implications for the design of an effective and efficient policy response to health insurance loss due to unemployment.

First, we examine the theoretic context of health insurance loss by the unemployed and then indicate empirical specifications for estimating both employed and unemployed worker demands for health insurance. We next estimate these relationships and discuss our findings; this is followed by our report on supplemental estimation from different data sources. We use our results next to simulate the loss of health insurance under historical economic conditions. Finally, we summarize our findings from this chapter.

THEORETIC CONSIDERATIONS

Consumers are believed to purchase health insurance because (1) their health status is uncertain, and (2) they dislike the resulting uncertainty of health care expenditures. The demand for health insurance emerges from a desire to reduce the financial risk occasioned by such uncertainty. More formally, consumers choose that amount of health insurance that maximizes expected utility over the distribution of alternative health status conditions, as shown in equation 4-1:

$$\text{Maximize } \int_h U[C, W+S, h+g(X, h)] \cdot f(h) \cdot dh \qquad \text{(Eq. 4-1)}$$

where $C = Y - P_I \cdot I - \gamma(I) \cdot X - S$, and variables are defined as follows:

  U is the ordinal utility function,
  C is the current expenditure on consumption (excluding health care expenditures),
  W is wealth,
  S is current savings (or dis-savings),
  h is the initial health status,
  X is the expenditure on health care services,
  g is the health production function (that is, the function for enhancing health status),
  f is the probability density function for h,
  Y is current income,
  I is the extent of health insurance,
  P_I is the price of health insurance,
  γ is the effective coinsurance rate.[1]

The consumer is portrayed as maximizing a function of consumption, C; final wealth, $W+S$; and final health status, $h+g(h, X)$. Because initial health status (h) is stochastically determined, the desired expenditure for health care services (X) is also stochastically determined,[2] and the risk-averse consumer purchases health insurance (I) to reduce the variability of total health care expense—including the cost of health insurance itself.

The theory of health insurance has received much attention in recent years and exegesis of theoretic representations, such as equation 4-1, has yielded a broad understanding such insurance demands.[3] For this reason we shall not pursue a fully comprehensive discussion of the underlying theoretic model. Instead we shall give special attention to those theoretic considerations that are particularly relevant to this study, particularly: (1) the effect on health insurance demand of the large and transitory income reductions associated with loss of employment, and (2) the interrelationship of group and individual insurance.

First, it seems unlikely, a priori, that previous analyses of the income effect generalize to the large and transitory income reductions associated with loss of employment. Income (Y) can be decomposed as

$$Y = Y_{normal} + Y_{transitory} \qquad \text{(Eq. 4-2)}$$

where Y_{normal} is normal or permanent income and $Y_{transitory}$ represents transitory or temporary deviations from normal income, and is negative in the case of unemployment. Permanent income theory and the life-cycle theory of consumption predict that a transitory decrease in income tends to be financed by dis-investment (or dis-saving).[4] This suggests that the loss of income associated with unemployment reduces the demand for health insurance less than would an equivalent decrease in normal or permanent income—that is, that $\partial I/\partial Y_{normal} > \partial I/\partial Y_{transitory}$ because $\partial S/\partial Y_{transitory} > \dfrac{\partial S}{\partial Y_{normal}}$ Thus, it seems unlikely that existing estimates of the income elasticity are appropriate for assessing the impact of job loss, and associated income loss, on the demand for health insurance. It is necessary to estimate a transitory income elasticity (or effect) for that purpose.

In addition to this (transitory) income effect, portrayed in Figure 4-1 as a downward shift in the demand curve, the loss of employment often entails a "price" effect, an upward shift in the supply curve in Figure 4-1. The loading fee for health insurance, defined as the excess of premiums over expected benefits, is often regarded as the price of insurance (Phelps 1973, pp. 47, 61-63). The loading fee or "price" of health insurance provided to large groups of consumers is substantially less—presumably because of economies of scale in marketing and administration—than the "price" for individually purchased health insurance.[5] Because almost all group health insurance is purchased through an employer, loss of employment can also entail loss of this group price advantage (as well as the price advantage due to tax exemption of employer-paid premiums), shifting the supply curve from S_{group} to $S_{individual}$ in Figure 4-1 and leading to a further reduction in the equilibrium level of health insurance. However, group health insurance from the former employer is not always lost during unemployment, as is

Figure 4-1
The Effect of Unemployment on the Demand for Health Insurance

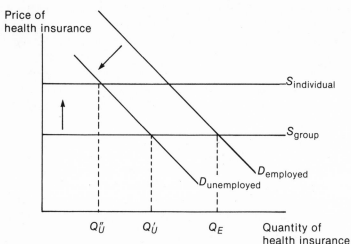

apparent from Chapter 3. In 1972 some 26 percent of unemployed household heads continued to receive group health insurance from their previous employers (see Table 3-1).[6] (Approximately 73 percent of employed household heads purchased group health insurance through their employer.)

We suggest that such continuation of group health insurance by the unemployed is significant and that any loss of group insurance by the unemployed is not fully arbitrary or capricious but rather that it reflects underlying economic factors. That is, unemployed workers continue to demand health insurance from their previous employer and that these unemployed worker demands partly determine the extent of continuation. Though this prospect may seem counterintuitive, it has become more credible given recent understanding of the importance of temporary layoffs in the theory of the firm. As Martin Feldstein (1975, 1976) asserts, the generally unnoticed fact that the typical worker who is laid off is soon rehired by his former employer requires a major reevaluation of current theories of unemployment. In particular, it suggests that temporary layoffs are part of the voluntary package of wages, hours, and work-sharing rules that employees choose or for which they bargain.

It does not seem unreasonable to suggest that the conditions of unemployment, including continuation of health insurance, are also part of this package. Thus, we predict that at least some unemployed workers continue to demand and purchase group health insurance from their previous employer, continuing to take advantage of the group price discount.[7] Nevertheless, not all unemployed workers have this opportunity, as will be shown.

Group health insurance typically has the (pure) public-good property of being available only in equal quantities, and qualities, to all persons within a group.[8] But because workers within a firm do not have homogeneous health needs or risk preference, and thus do not have the same demands for health insurance, the kind or quantity of group health insurance available through the firm will differ from that demanded for at least some workers. Figure 4-2 portrays the demands for health insurance of three different workers within the same firm. The ith, jth and kth individuals demand, respectively, Q_i, Q_j and Q_k of group health insurance. Suppose that Q_{group}, equal to Q_j, is the quantity provided by the firm. If so, the ith individual will be receiving more than he wanted; and the kth individual will be receiving less than he wanted. That is, the quantity demanded will not equal the quantity provided for all or most individuals.

We shall assume that the fixed level of group health insurance, Q_{group} is determined as the mean quantity demanded—that is, the average of individual demands for health insurance is

$$Q_{\text{group}} = \sum_{i=1,n} \frac{Q_i^D}{n} = \sum_{i=1,n} \frac{D(X_i)}{n} \qquad \text{(Eq. 4-3)}$$

where $Q_i^D = D(X_i)$ is the quantity of health insurance demanded by the ith individual who has X_i characteristics.[9] Thus, individual demands will be distributed as

$$Q_{\text{group}} = Q_i^D + v_i = D(X_i) + v_i \qquad \text{(Eq. 4-4)}$$

where v_i is a variable that has zero mean and that measures the extent to which the quantity of group health insurance deviates from the individual demands. This form is empirically convenient because it will permit us to estimate the $D(X_i)$ health insurance demand function from data on the group health insurance coverage of individual workers. Consider that

Figure 4–2

The Distribution of Demands for Group Health Insurance Within a Group

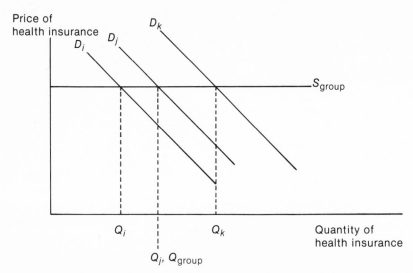

Figure 4–3

The Residual Demand for Individual Health Insurance

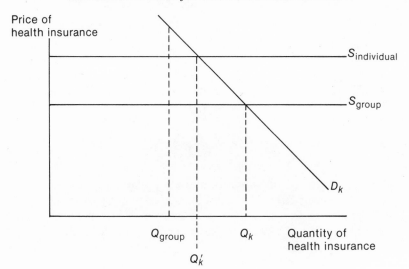

the demand for health insurance is a classical normal linear regression model

$$Q_i^D = \alpha + \beta X_i + \epsilon_i \qquad \text{(Eq. 4-5)}$$

where the stochastic disturbance ϵ_i is normally distributed with zero mean. Then substituting (4-5) into (4-4) obtains

$$Q_{\text{group}} = Q_i^D + v_i = \alpha + \beta X_i + \epsilon_i + v_i \qquad \text{(Eq. 4-6)}$$
$$= \alpha + \beta X_i + \eta_i$$

where $\eta_i = \epsilon_i + v_i$. Assuming that v_i is normal and that it is independent of ϵ_i, η_i is normally distributed with zero mean and can be viewed as a random variable that behaves precisely like ϵ_i. Thus, equation 4-6 is formally equivalent to the classical regression model in equation 4-5, and its least-squares estimators will have the desirable properties (see Kmenta 1971, pp. 314-15, for further discussion). That is, the health insurance demand function can be estimated by ordinary least squares (OLS) from group health insurance data, despite the "error" in that variable.[10]

The above model of group health insurance determination also provides the raison d'etre for individual health insurance. Given unrestricted choice between group and individual insurance it may be assumed that one would always choose the lower-priced group insurance. However, as we have seen, the choice is not unconstrained. If the kth individual in Figure 4-2 can obtain only Q_{group} of group insurance, he will be undersatisfied and will wish to supplement this quantity of health insurance— that is, he will have a residual demand for health insurance equal to $Q_k - Q_{\text{group}}$ in Figure 4-3. Because, by assumption, he cannot purchase additional group health insurance, this demand may be expected to spill over into the market for individual insurance. However, because of the higher price of individual health insurance, the quantity bought— $Q_k' - Q_{\text{group}}$ in Figure 4-3—will be less than the residual quantity demanded at the group price— $Q_k - Q_{\text{group}}$ in Figure 4-3. Of course, if no health insurance is provided by the employer—if $Q_{\text{group}} = 0$—the entire demand for health insurance spills over into the individual health insurance market.

It is further significant that the disequilibrium adjustment mechanism is not symmetric. Though the undersatisfied kth individual in Figure 4-2 can supplement group insurance through purchase of individual insurance, the oversatisfied ith individual does not have any comparable mechanism for reducing health insurance coverage.[11] Thus, we predict that i-type individuals will tend to remain over insured and therefore that the population is overinsured in the aggregate. This prediction has two implications for our study:

1. The actual demand for health insurance cannot be reliably estimated by taking total health insurance, group and individual combined, as the dependent variable. All coefficient estimates would be biased toward zero because the covariance between the dependent variable and η_i in equation 4-6 is known to be negative. Again, demand estimation from group health insurance holdings does not confront this problem.

2. The actual loss of health insurance by the unemployed may overstate the extent of the problem because some of the unemployed were overinsured, in an efficiency sense, while employed.

Although the existing theory of health insurance is reasonably well developed and has been used as a guide for empirical specification in the next section, the extant theory was not adequate for our purpose. Thus, we have sought in this section to identify and expand our understanding of those theoretic considerations which are especially important in studying loss of health insurance due to unemployment.

DETERMINANTS OF DEMAND FOR HEALTH INSURANCE—EMPIRICAL SPECIFICATION

In this section we indicate the empirical specifications for estimating the health insurance demand function, $Q_i^D = D(X_i)$, which was discussed in the preceding section. In fact, we propose to estimate two such functions—one for the employed and one for the unemployed—and thereby to allow for complete interaction between work status and all other independent variables. Such interaction is potentially important for at least two reasons:

1. Despite our attempt to control for observable differences between the employed and the unemployed, it seems likely that some differences between them are unobservable and that these differences may bias the estimation. In particular, unemployed persons tend to have a lower health status than employed persons and, all else being equal, may demand more health insurance.

2. Because unemployment typically entails a large income reduction it may not be appropriate to assume—as would have to be done if we estimated only one function for both employed and unemployed workers—that the intensity of demographic-related preferences does not vary with income. In particular, it seems probable that demographic-related preferences for health insurance would be more important at a "high," employed income level than at a "low," unemployed income level.

Estimating health insurance demand functions confronts some important data limitations. Only one data source, the Pension Plan and Health Insurance (PPHI) supplement to the 1972 Current Population Survey (CPS), reported all of the following[12]—(1) length of time unemployed (for those unemployed); (2) data sufficient to estimate weekly earnings while employed; and (3) work-group size.[13] Each of these variables is important in estimating a correctly specified model. However, the PPHI data may also have several distinct disadvantages. First, it is 1972 data and therefore may be out of date. Second, PPHI only requested data on group health insurance coverage and does not have information on individually purchased health insurance. But recall that our theoretic discussion has established that the health insurance demand functions can be estimated from data on the group health insurance coverage of individual workers and that estimation from total health insurance coverage information may in fact yield biased results (see the previous section). Finally, PPHI's information on group health insurance coverage is dichotomous. It indicates whether or not somebody has group health insurance but does not discriminate differences in insurance "quality." Despite these misgivings, PPHI seems to be the most appropriate data base for our study, although we will conduct supplemental analyses from two other data sources—the 1970 CHAS-NORC Survey of Health Services Expenditure Utilization and the 1975–76 CHAS-NORC Medical Access Study—which do not have quite the same limitations.

We shall assume that the general demand relationship between group health insurance coverage, and household characteristics can be expressed as in equation 4–7:

$$\text{GHI} = F \text{ (PINC, NTRANS, GRP1, GRP2, EDUC, AGE, RACE, SEX, MSTAT, NCHILD, RES, IND1–IND8, COST)}$$

(Eq. 4–7)

where the dependent variable (GHI) is a 0–1 indicator of group health insurance coverage and the independent variables are characteristics of the household and household head. (Variables are defined in Table 4–1.) We have used the existing theory of reimbursement health insurance as a guide to specification of this model. However, the model also reflects the special theoretic considerations discussed in the previous section. In particular, the income reductions associated with loss of employment (NTRANS) are viewed as being transitory and distinguished from variation in full employment income (PINC), a more nearly permanent income construct.[14]

The work-group size variables (GRP1 and GRP2) are regarded as instrumental variables for the "price" or loading fee of health insurance, because group discounts on health insurance increase with the contract size.[15] The age (AGE), education (EDUC), race (RACE), sex (SEX), marital status (MSTAT), number of children (NCHILD), and residence (RES) variables were included for two reasons: to proxy systematic individual variation in risk preference, and to proxy similar variation in the risk itself (that is, variation in the health care expenditure). All else equal, health care expense is known to increase with age and education, and to be greater for whites, females, married households, households with more children, and urban residents.[16] Unfortunately, the effects of these same variables on risk preference are not so well known, and we cannot indicate hypotheses as to their overall effect. Nevertheless there seems to be a general presumption in the literature that the health expenditure effect predominates. The industry variables (IND1 – IND8) were included to proxy institutional variation in the availability of health insurance.[17]

The self-employment variable (CLASS) may serve several functions. Because self-employment is inherently more risky (in terms of chances for success), self-employed workers may be less risk-averse in general and hence may demand less health insurance. In addition, self-employment may signal that the work-group size is very small—that is, CLASS can be regarded as a further instrumental variable for the "price" of health insurance. The COST variable is meant to proxy regional variation in the cost of health care.[18] Such variation may result from any of the following factors: (1) price differences, (2) differences in the distribution of illness, and (3) differences in utilization patterns. Therefore, we hypothesize that the demand for health insurance varies directly with COST.

Because the dependent variable (GHI in equation 4–7) is dichotomous, the classic assumption of homoskedastic or constant variance

Table 4-1 Identification of Variables

GHI—Dummy variable indicating group health insurance coverage status
  0—does not have group health insurance
  1—has group health insurance

PINC—Proxy for permanent income (head's weekly wage times 52 plus other family income, excluding unemployment compensation)

NTRANS—Proxy for *negative* transitory income (head's weekly wage times number of weeks unemployed, excluding unemployment compensation)

Work-Group
Size[a]—Dummy variables indicating
  GRP1—25–99 persons
  GRP2—100 or more persons

EDUC—Years of schooling completed (a proxy for education)

AGE—Age in years

RACE—Dummy variable indicating race
  0—white
  1—non-white

SEX—Dummy variable indicating sex
  0—male
  1—female

NCHILD—Number of children under 18

RES—Dummy variable indicating residence
  0—urban
  1—rural

MSTAT—Dummy variable indicating marital status
  0—single
  1—married

Industry[b]—Dummy variables indicating
  IND1—Agriculture and private household
  IND2—Mining
  IND3—Construction
  IND4—Manufacturing
  IND5—Transportation
  IND6—Wholesale and retail trade
  IND7—Finance, insurance, and real estate
  IND8—Public administration

CLASS—Dummy variable indicating class of work
  0—not self-employed
  1—self-employed

COST—Proxy for regional variation in the cost of health care (total per capita personal health care expenditure, by Census Division, 1969)

Source: All variables (except COST)—April 1972 CPS and PPHI supplement; COST—U.S. Department of Health, Education and Welfare, *Personal Health Care Expenditures by State* (Washington, D.C.: Government Printing Office, 1975).

[a]Under 25 persons is the omitted category.

[b]Miscellaneous services is the omitted category.

residuals is not valid and ordinary-least-squares regression is not entirely appropriate (Goldberger, 1964, p. 249). Although various procedures have been recommended as alternatives, the Probit model is most common. In the Probit model it is considered that an index I, which has the standardized normal distribution, is a linear function of the regressors (that is, $I = b^0 + b_1 \text{ EDUC} + b_2 \text{ AGE} + \ldots$). The conditional expectation (in this case, the probability of having health insurance) is then given by the ordinate of the cumulative normal distribution that falls in the unit or 0–1 interval and forms and S-shaped curve as shown in Figure 4–4. For example, a predicted value of I equal to $+1.0$ implies that the probability of having group health insurance is 84.1 percent, because that is the probability of being one standard deviation above the mean. We will estimate the GHI relationship in equation 4–7 as a Probit model. However, we also estimate it by ordinary least squares (OLS), because OLS results are more readily interpretable.

Figure 4–4
The Transformation of the Dependent Variable in Probit Analysis

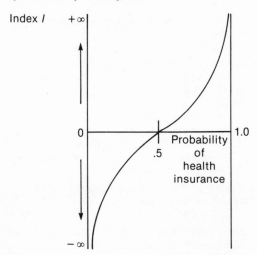

RESULTS OF ESTIMATION AND DISCUSSION

The results of estimating health insurance demands separately for the employed and the unemployed, using both Probit and OLS (ordinary least squares) procedures, are shown in Table 4-2.[19] All models yielded highly significant equations, and in each case the hypothesis of no relationship between GHI and the independent variable list (that is, that $b_1 = b_2 = \ldots = 0$) can be rejected at better than the .10 level. Nine of the 19 independent variables (excluding NTRANS) were significant at the .10 level or better in the Probit estimation of health insurance demands of the employed; 8 of the 19 variables were significant in the OLS estimation. Regarding unemployed worker demands, 8 of the 20 independent variables (including NTRANS) were significant in the Probit estimation, and 10 of the 20 variables were significant in OLS estimation.

Because of the nonlinear transformation involved in Probit analysis (see the previous section), we cannot easily discern the quantitative importance of the Probit coefficients from the parameter estimates reported in Table 4-2. For this reason we have used the estimated Probit model to predict the effect on the probability of having health insurance of variation in each of the independent variables, taking other variables at their mean values. For example, Table 4-3 shows that as permanent income (PINC) rises from $6,000 per year to $10,000 the probability of having health insurance increases by 3.5 percentage points for the employed worker and by 7.2 percentage points for the unemployed worker. It also shows that employment in the construction industry (IND3) is associated with a 14.2 percentage point lower probability of group health insurance than employment in the miscellaneous services industry. To facilitate comparison of the Probit and OLS models, the OLS-estimated effects are also shown in Table 4-3.[20]

The Probit and OLS results are qualitatively similar in that the signs of coefficients are almost always the same in parallel models and the same variables tend to be significant. Furthermore, both techniques estimate quantitatively similar effects for at least a majority of the independent variables, although it is apparent that the two models yield substantially different estimates of the quantitative effect for some variables (for example, GRP1, SEX, IND1, and IND8).

Both models strongly support the hypothesis from the last section that at least some unemployed workers continue to demand group health insurance from their previous employer. In particular, continuation of group health insurance during unemployment is shown to be systemat-

Table 4-2 The Demands for Health Insurance by Work Status of Household Head, 1972—Probit and OLS Parameter Estimates

Independent Variable	Probit Model		OLS Model	
	Employed (N = 802)	Unemployed (N = 260)	Employed (N = 802)	Unemployed (N = 260)
Constant	− .359 (− .542)	− 4.25* (− 3.40)	.481* (3.78)	− .641* (− 1.93)
PINC (permanent income)	.0000331* (2.46)	.0000726* (3.56)	.00000637* (2.54)	.0000210* (3.61)
NTRANS (negative transitory income)	—	− .000102* (− 2.69)	—	− .0000276* (− 2.78)
Work-group size[a]				
GRP1 (25–99 persons)	.560* (3.26)	1.64* (2.20)	.171* (4.52)	.505* (2.26)
GRP2 (100 or more persons)	1.18* (7.10)	1.33* (2.08)	.246* (7.78)	.382* (2.10)
EDUC (education)	.0272 (1.16)	.0790* (2.14)	.00686 (1.53)	.0191* (1.89)
AGE (age)	− .000496 (− .0909)	− .000158 (− .0199)	− .000257 (− .240)	.000615 (.276)
RACE (non-white)	− .508* (− 2.24)	.576* (1.88)	− .116* (− 2.24)	.149* (1.83)
SEX (female)	− .223 (− .854)	− .374 (− .804)	− .04711 (− .862)	− .0134 (− .122)
NCHILD (number of children)	.102* (2.49)	− .0122 (− .215)	.0183* (2.46)	− .00481 (− .312)
RES (rural residence)	− .143 (− .936)	− .456* (− 2.04)	− .0335 (− 1.13)	− .127* (− 2.01)
MSTAT (married)	.134 (.56)	.405 (1.30)	.037 (.79)	.128 (1.43)
Industry[b]				
IND1 (agriculture and private household)	− .387 (− 1.19)	− 1.89* (− 5.50)	− .167* (− 2.44)	.0292 (.154)
IND2 (mining)	2.70 (1.24)	2.57* (3.23)	.205 (1.59)	.760* (3.32)
IND3 (construction)	− .462* (− 1.94)	1.05* (2.77)	− .144* (− 2.78)	.265* (2.91)

Table 4-2 *continued*

Independent Variable	Probit Model		OLS Model	
	Employed (N = 802)	Unemployed (N = 260)	Employed (N = 802)	Unemployed (N = 260)
IND4 (manufacturing)	.362* (1.87)	.752* (2.03)	.0564 (1.59)	.177* (2.01)
IND5 (transtation and public utilities)	.275 (1.06)	.423 (.841)	.0460 (.958)	.0969 (.740)
IND6 (wholesale and retail trade)	.165 (.838)	.521 (1.20)	.0236 (.564)	.120 (1.18)
IND7 (finance, insurance and real estate)	.598* (1.80)	−2.16 (−.636)	.0874 (1.59)	−.120 (−.680)
IND8 (public administration)	−.589* (−1.71)	−2.65 (−.631)	−.122 (−1.60)	−.197 (−.864)
CLASS (self-employed)	−1.21 (−5.91)	.00488 (.00963)	−.383* (−8.35)	.0333 (.224)
COST (regional cost index)	−.0000539 (−.284)	.00126 (.409)	−.0000445 (−.125)	.0000765 (.0919)
Coefficient of determination (R^2)			.387	.219
Corrected Coefficient of Determination			.371	.150
F-ratio			24.6	3.18
Log likelihood ratio	−401	−34.2		
Significance level F-ratio or log likelihood ratio	<.01	<.01	<.001	<.001

Note: *Significant at .10 level. *t* statistics in parentheses.

[a] Under 25 persons is the omitted category.

[b] Miscellaneous services is the omitted category.

Table 4-3   Simulating the Effect of Variation in the Independent Variables

Variable Identification and Values	Effect on the Probability of Having Group Health Insurance (percentages)			
	Employed		Unemployed	
	Probit Model	OLS Model	Probit Model	OLS Model
Permanent income (PINC)				
6,000	0	0	0	0
8,000	+ 1.7	+ 1.3	+ 3.3	+ 4.2
10,000	+ 3.5	+ 2.6	+ 7.2	+ 8.4
12,000	+ 4.9	+ 3.8	+ 11.5	+ 12.6
15,000	+ 7.0	+ 7.3	+ 17.8	+ 18.9
20,000	+ 9.9	+ 8.9	+ 22.6	+ 29.4
Negative transitory income (NTRANS)				
0	—	—	0	0
1,000	—	—	− 3.5	− 2.8
2,000	—	—	− 6.6	− 5.5
3,000	—	—	− 9.8	− 8.28
4,000	—	—	− 12.3	− 11.0
5,000	—	—	− 14.8	− 13.8
Work-group size (a proxy for price)				
Under 25 persons (omitted category)	0	0	0	0
25–99 persons (GRP1)	+ 10.0	+ 17.1	+ 45.0	+ 50.5
100 or more persons (GRP2)	+ 27.6	+ 24.6	+ 37.7	+ 38.2
Education (EDUC)				
10	0	0	0	0
12	+ 1.2	+ 1.4	+ 4.5	+ 3.8
14	+ 2.4	+ 2.7	+ 9.6	+ 7.6
16	+ 3.5	+ 4.1	+ 14.1	+ 11.5
18	+ 4.6	+ 5.5	+ 21.1	+ 15.3
20	+ 5.6	+ 6.9	+ 27.3	+ 19.1
Age (AGE)				
20	0	0	0	0
30	− 0.2	− 0.3	0	+ 0.6
40	− 0.3	− 0.5	0	+ 1.2
50	− 0.4	− 0.8	− 0.1	+ 1.8
60	− 0.5	− 1.0	− 0.1	+ 2.5
Nonwhite (RACE)	− 13.8	− 11.6	+ 19.5	+ 14.9
Female (SEX)	− 5.3	− 4.7	− 10.0	− 1.3

Table 4-3 *continued*

Variable Identification and Values	Effect on the Probability of Having Group Health Insurance (percentages)			
	Employed		Unemployed	
	Probit Model	OLS Model	Probit Model	OLS Model
Number of children (NCHILD)				
0	0	0	0	0
1	+ 2.5	+ 1.8	− 0.4	− 0.5
2	+ 4.7	+ 3.6	− 0.7	− 1.0
3	+ 6.8	+ 5.5	− 1.1	− 1.4
4	+ 8.5	+ 7.3	− 1.5	− 1.9
5	+ 10.1	+ 9.1	− 1.8	− 2.4
Rural Residence (RES)				
	− 3.3	− 3.3	− 11.2	− 12.7
Industry				
Miscellaneous Services (omitted category)	0	0	0	0
Agriculture and Private Household (IND1)	− 11.6	− 16.7	− 11.1	+ 2.9
Mining (IND2)	+ 17.2	+ 20.5	+ 79.0	+ 76.0
Construction (IND3)	− 14.2	− 14.4	+ 29.8	+ 26.5
Manufacturing (IND4)	+ 7.7	+ 5.6	+ 18.7	+ 17.7
Transportation and Public Utilities (IND5)	+ 7.1	+ 4.6	+ 8.5	+ 9.7
Wholesale and Retail Trade (IND6)	+ 3.9	+ 2.4	+ 11.3	+ 12.0
Finance, Insurance and Real Estate (IND7)	+ 11.1	+ 8.7	− 11.1	− 12.0
Public Administration (IND8)	− 18.7	− 12.2	− 11.1	− 19.7
Self-employed (CLASS)	− 38.2	− 38.3	+ 0.1	+ 3.3
Regional cost index (COST)				
200	0	0	0	0
225	− 0.3	− 0.1	+ 1.0	+ 0.2
250	− 0.6	− 0.2	+ 1.8	+ 0.4
275	− 0.9	− 0.3	+ 2.8	+ 0.6
300	− 1.2	− 0.4	+ 3.8	+ 0.8

ically (and significantly) related to the income and price variables as well as other demographic characteristics. With the exception of NCHILD, the estimated quantitative effects in Table 4-3 are greater for the un- employed than for the employed, even though the percentage of variance explained is greater for the employed. We conclude that loss of group health insurance by the unemployed is not fully arbitrary or capricious, but rather it reflects underlying economic factors. The quantitative importance of continuation is another matter—and one that we shall examine after brief consideration of the other findings.

As suggested in the last section, existing estimates of the income elasticity of demand for health insurance are not appropriate for assess- ing the impact of the large and transitory income reductions associated with loss of employment; it is also necessary to estimate a transitory income elasticity (or effect) for that purpose. We then estimated separate coefficients (in Table 4-2) for the permanent and transitory components of income, taking the loss of income due to unemployment as our proxy for negative transitory income. Though the separate coefficients are both highly significant, we find that, contrary to permanent income theory, the coefficient for negative transitory income (NTRANS) is larger in absolute value than the one for permanent income (PINC). This seeming anomaly may, however, be more apparent than real. The NTRANS vari- able is based on an uncompleted episode of unemployment and does not reflect either the expectation of further income loss due to continuation of a single episode or the prospect of subsequent unemployment episodes in the same year. The average duration of unemployment at time of sur- vey had been 12 weeks in our 1972 PPHI sample. We estimate from 1969 data that the expectation of continued unemployment at that point is 10.5 weeks.[21] Thus, it seems that we have, on the average, underestimated transitory income by at least 87.5 percent $(10.5/12 \times 100)$ and that the coefficient for NTRANS is overestimated by an equivalent percentage. If the NTRANS coefficients are adjusted accordingly, we obtain $-.000544$ as the NTRANS coefficient in the Probit model and $-.0000147$ in the OLS model. These coefficients are now, as predicted, considerably less in absolute value than the coefficients estimated for PINC, although the differences between NTRANS and PINC coefficients are not significant.

The work-group size variables (GRP1 and GRP2) were regarded as instrumental variables for the price or loading fee of health insurance, because group discounts on health insurance increase with the contract size. Thus, our finding in Table 4-2 that all GRP1 and GRP2 coefficients are significant and positive constitutes evidence that the quantity of health insurance increases as price decreases, for both employed and unemployed. This usual price effect is further supported for the employed because the GRP2 coefficients significantly (.10 level or better) exceed the GRP1 coefficients. However, considering the unemployed only, we find that GRP1 coefficients exceed the GRP2 coefficients, although the differences are "small" and not significant. Either the associated price difference is less important for the unemployed, or, more likely, the data limitations here (see note 13) have biased the results.

Although formal hypotheses were not indicated for the other demographic variables, there was a general presumption that the demand for health insurance would increase with age, education, and number of children and be greater for whites, females, married households, and urban residents. For both employed and unemployed these informal expectations are borne out with respect to education and residence. However, it is noteworthy that the coefficients are larger in absolute value and more significant for the unemployed. Some of the other results are more difficult to understand.

The demand for health insurance is estimated to increase significantly with number of children for the employed, but not for the unemployed. The NCHILD coefficents for the unemployed are negative and lack significance. It may be that the immediate financial "need" of a large family with an unemployed head dominates the greater risk attached to having no health insurance.

Perhaps even more surprising is that the demand for health insurance does not vary significantly or importantly with age. The following is suggested as a possible rationale for this anomalous finding. The dependent variable in our analysis is group health insurance, which is assumed to be determined as the average of individual demands for health insurance. Thus, age could be an important determinant of health insurance demands, but if work groups tend to have a similar distribution of ages, as seems possible, there might not be sufficient age-related variation across groups to permit reliable estimation of the effect. In any event this finding merits further investigation.

The estimation of negative, although insignificant, coefficients for the SEX variable may result from a similar artifact of the present linkage between workplace and purchase of health insurance. Most working women are married and family health insurance tends to be provided in the context of husband's employment. Thus, we predict that women's demand for health insurance will be low and that the level of group health insurance provided will reflect this lower level of demand. To the extent that female heads (nonmarried females) work in the same places, they may tend to be underinsured, biasing downwards our estimates of the SEX coefficient. This happens because the health insurance demand of the average female head is different from that for the average female worker, including both heads and nonheads.

The coefficients estimated for RACE (nonwhite) are also difficult to understand. As anticipated, employed nonwhites are estimated to have a significantly lower demand for health insurance than otherwise similar employed whites. However, unemployed nonwhites have a significantly greater demand for health insurance. We cannot, at present, explain this dramatic reversal, unless the greater incidence of unemployment among nonwhites (see Appendix A) prompts them to make better institutional arrangements for continuing health insurance during unemployment.

The results in Tables 4-2 and 4-3 indicate that the provision of group health insurance strongly depends on the industry of employment (the IND1–IND8 variables), even after controlling for variation in other worker characteristics. If our demand relationships are otherwise correctly specified, the estimated importance of interindustry variation may be viewed as signaling a market failure in providing group health insurance in that the provision of group health insurance depends importantly on institutional arrangements unrelated to demand variation. (Some of the findings above also suggest an institutional market failure—e.g., the findings with respect to the SEX variable.) For example, the pattern of coefficients for IND1 through IND8 may be explained in part by interindustry differences in unionization. Mining (IND2) and manufacturing (IND3), both highly unionized industries, are estimated to have the highest levels of group health insurance, while public administration (IND8) and agriculture and private household (IND1), largely nonunionized industries, are estimated to have the lowest levels.

Some other industries—transportation and public utilities (IND5), wholesale and retail trade (IND6), and miscellaneous services (the omitted category)—fall in between, much as might be predicted by this unionization hypothesis. However, the results for the construction (IND2) and finance, insurance, and real estate (IND7) industries require further explanation. As predicted, workers in the highly unionized construction industry have a high level of health insurance while unemployed. However, contrary to expectation, they are estimated to have a lower level while employed. This result possibly reflects the tendency of construction unions to withhold benefits until someone has worked a minimum period of time, a mechanism for excluding summer or other casual employees from benefits. Finally, the unexpectedly high level of health insurance in finance, insurance, and real estate (IND7), a non-unionized industry, may reflect the lower costs of providing insurance to insurance workers.

We had predicted that the self-employed (CLASS) would have less health insurance. The results indicate that the self-employed have significantly less health insurance while employed but that the level of health insurance is not so different among the unemployed. This might reflect the greater ease with which these self-employed workers who did have health insurance can continue it during unemployment.

Findings for COST, the regional cost index, were unexpected. The coefficients estimated for this variable were uniformly and highly insignificant. Although this suggests that regional differences in the provision of group health insurance are apparently unrelated to regional variation in the cost of health care, our index of regional cost variation has been measured very crudely.

We now return to the issue raised earlier in this section—the quantitative importance of group health insurance continuation during unemployment. Our analysis has shown that at least some unemployed workers continue to demand group health insurance from their previous employer and that continuation of health insurance during unemployment is significantly related to economic and other demographic factors. We now wish to ask how well these factors account for the actual magnitude of health insurance loss among the unemployed. The answer seems to be that only a small fraction of this magnitude is explained by our modeling effort.

For example, by substituting the mean characteristics of the unemployed into the Probit unemployed equation, we find that the typical unemployed person has a 22.4 percent probability of having group health insurance. If negative transitory income (NTRANS) is set equal to zero, this probability only rises to 29.9 percent, a 7.5 percentage point increase. If the characteristics of the unemployed are substituted into the Probit employed equation, we estimate an 83.4 percent probability of having health insurance, compared to 86.3 percent for the employed. Thus, the loss of income due to unemployment explains only $7.5/(83.4 - 22.4)$ or 12.3 percent of the total health insurance loss.[22] How then do we account for the remaining 88 percent of this health insurance gap—the difference between 83.4 and 29.9, or 53.5 percentage points? Although it is not possible to give a definitive answer, we can indicate several alternatives.

First, our econometric approach explicitly accommodates any differences between the employed and the unemployed in their "taste" for health insurance—namely, by estimating separate equations for the employed and unemployed. That is, some relevant differences between the employed and the unemployed are either not observable or were not available for our modeling effort. If such differences are important, it may not be fully appropriate to estimate the probability of an unemployed worker having had health insurance while employed by using the equation for the employed estimated here. Nevertheless, it seems unlikely that any deficiencies in the demand estimation can account for a very substantial portion of the 53.5 percentage point gap in probability of health insurance.[23]

The alternative explanation of this gap is much more compelling. It is that many unemployed workers simply do not have the opportunity to continue group health insurance provided by their previous employer. Either the employer is insensitive to the demands for continuation of health insurance during unemployment, or the employed workers themselves are insensitive to the possibility of unemployment and fail to transmit their "true" demands by negotiating for continuation of group health insurance during unemployment. This may be efficient, particularly in jobs where unemployment is not common. Although loss of group health insurance does not preclude the purchase of individual health insurance, the sharply higher (70–80 percent) price of individual insurance implies that that kind of adjustment is not a very satisfactory alternative; the coefficients obtained for the unemployed in the GRP1 and GRP2 "price" variables signal that the price elasticity is large.

In fact, as Chapter 3 indicates, only a small percentage of unemployed workers without group health insurance choose to substitute individual insurance. For this reason, the level of health insurance among the unemployed may be inefficiently too low (or suboptimal), assuming that the employer's group price in fact represents the (social) marginal cost of continuing the insurance. (This issue is also examined in Chapter 5.) Thus, we attribute much of the unemployment-related reduction in health insurance to a health insurance market failure. The reduction seems to be an artifact of the predominant work-group institutional mechanism for financing health insurance in our country and bears little or no relation to underlying demand and cost considerations.

SUPPLEMENTAL ESTIMATION

In this section we use essentially the same model developed above to estimate the employed and unemployed health insurance demands from two different data sources, the 1970 CHAS-NORC (CHAS) Survey of Health Services Utilization and Expenditure and the 1975–76 CHAS-NORC Medical Access Study (MAS). (See Chapter 3 for a brief discussion of both data sources.) Such independent replication of the analysis is important to establish the validity or stability of a relationship. Furthermore, any changes in parameter estimates over time may be useful in diagnosing structural shifts in the behavioral relationship itself—that is, systematic changes in health insurance demands not accounted for by the model. However, these were not the main purposes for supplemental estimation. Each of the alternative data sources has important advantages over the 1972 PPHI analyzed above; these advantages permit us to explore several variations on the basic model and thereby to give a more comprehensive analysis. In addition, the CHAS data are substantially validated and the MAS data are more current than PPHI. However, CHAS and MAS also have significant limitations that PPHI did not— most notably "small" sample sizes for the unemployed.

The Demands for Group Health Insurance

We begin by considering the group health insurance demand equations shown in the first four columns of Table 4-4. Both employed and unemployed "group" equations were estimated by OLS (ordinary least squares) from both data sources. Except for the following changes in variable definition or specification of the independent variable list, the relationships are the same as the OLS-estimated equations in Table 4-2.

1. Instead of using work group size categories as a proxy for the price of health insurance, an instrumental variable technique has been used to estimate a price variable, PRICE, as the ratio between the premium amount and the expected value of benefits.[24] That is, PRICE is defined as being equal to one plus the "loading" fraction.

Table 4-4 The Demands for Health Insurance by Work Status of Household Head, 1970 and 1975–76, OLS Parameter Estimates

	Group Equations				Nongroup Equations			
	Employed		Unemployed		Employed		Unemployed	
Independent Variable	(1) CHAS (N=1373)	(2) MAS (N=2263)	(3) CHAS (N=102)	(4) MAS (N=146)	(5) CHAS (N=429)	(6) MAS (N=489)	(7) CHAS (N=79)	(8) MAS (N=97)
Constant	3.92	4.24	4.12	.548	−.114	−.433	−.0662	−.380
PINC (permanent income)	.00000951* (4.78)	.00000778* (6.79)	.0000379* (3.05)	.0000153* (1.77)	.00000572 (1.46)	−.00000613* (1.96)	.00000114 (.096)	.0000156* (1.96)
NTRANS (negative transitory income)		.00000630* (−7.39)	.0000100 (−.446)	−.0000260* (−3.25)		−.0000710* (−3.36)	.0000393* (1.94)	−.0000180* (−2.03)
PRICE (price index)	−3.36* (−2.33)	−3.43* (−3.46)	−3.90 (−.818)	−.721 (−.126)				
EDUC (education)	.0141* (3.49)	.01916* (7.04)	−.0317* (−2.05)	−.000636 (−.447)	.00957 (1.20)	.0233* (3.74)	.00882 (.581)	.0252* (1.98)
AGE (age)	.00252* (2.37)	.00226* (2.76)	.00850* (2.58)	−.000167 (−.045)	.00568* (2.88)	.0105* (4.71)	.00370 (1.15)	.0154* (4.12)
RACE (nonwhite)	−.0692* (−2.25)	−.0326 (−1.36)	.113 (1.16)	.196* (2.07)	−.176* (−2.81)	.0923 (1.58)	−.0592 (−.633)	.207* (2.14)
SEX (female)	−.0427 (−.824)	−.0202 (−1.28)	−.00613 (−.0494)	−.0734 (−.956)	.0697 (.720)	.0720* (1.66)	.231* (1.93)	−.0543 (−.646)
NCHILD (number of children)	−.0106 (−1.56)	−.0162* (−2.91)	−.0280 (−1.30)	.00632 (.263)	−.000965 (−.075)	−.00133 (−.105)	−.0344* (−1.66)	−.0119 (−.471)

Table 4-4 *continued*

Residence[a]

	(1)	(2)	(3)	(4)	(5)	(6)	(7)	(8)
RES 1 (SMSA, central city)	-.0129 (-.421)		-.0351 (-.325)		-.0271 (-.400)		-.0810 (-.770)	
RES 2 (non-SMSA)	-.0155 (-.483)		-.0379 (-.317)		.0597 (.895)		.0360 (.302)	
SMSA (SMSA residence)		-.0204 (-1.11)		-.0229 (-.237)		.0403 (.751)		-.0967 (.913)
MSTAT (married)	.0641 (1.43)	.0310 (1.40)	-.0596 (-.551)	.163 (1.54)	-.0163 (-.182)	.0333 (.592)	-.0303 (-.294)	.0109 (.126)

Industry[b]

	(1)	(2)	(3)	(4)
IND1 (agriculture and private household)	-.196* (-2.66)	-.176* (-3.31)	-.140 (-.614)	.225 (.912)
IND2 (mining)	.127 (.911)	-.00712 (-.126)	c	c
IND3 (construction)	.0285 (.470)	.0325 (-.945)	-.0168 (-.112)	.270* (1.71)
IND4 (manufacturing)	.144* (3.00)	.0356 (1.12)	.0638 (.415)	.278 (1.51)
IND5 (transportation and public utilities)	.0663 (.800)	-.0798 (-1.43)	-.447 (-1.42)	.197 (6.07)
IND6 (wholesale and retail trade)	.0180 (.463)	.0127 (.457)	-.0283 (-.216)	.104 (.752)
IND7 (finance, insurance and real estate)	.00271 (.041)	-.116* (-2.36)	c	.480 (1.34)

Note: t statistics in parentheses.

*Significant at .10 level or better.

Table 4-4 *continued*

| | Group Equations | | | | Nongroup Equations | | | |
| | Employed | | Unemployed | | Employed | | Unemployed | |
Independent Variable	*(1) CHAS* (N=1373)	*(2) MAS* (N=2263)	*(3) CHAS* (N=102)	*(4) MAS* (N=146)	*(5) CHAS* (N=429)	*(6) MAS* (N=489)	*(7) CHAS* (N=79)	*(8) MAS* (N=97)
IND8 (public administration)	-.0592 (-.813)	-.164* (-3.24)	-.0813 (-.285)	-.292 (-.873)				
CLASS (self-employed)	-.360* (-9.15)	-.396* (15.3)	.0742 (-.452)	-.185 (-.904)				
COST (regional cost index)	.000791* (2.65)	.000215 (.904)	.00111 (.962)	.000769 (.713)	.000572 (.928)	-.0000238 (-.0316)	-.000261 (-.243)	-.000993 (-.850)
SPOUSE EMPSTAT (working wife)				.0910 (.818)				
Health Status[d]								
HSTAT1 (better than average for age)		-.0167 (-1.00)		.0102 (.110)		-.0653 (-1.42)		-.0940 (-1.04)
HSTAT2 (worse than average for age)		-.0979* (-2.78)		-.0880 (-.787)		-.131* (-1.70)		-.128 (-1.15)
Coefficient of determination (R^2)	.232	.226	.403	.325	.092	.120	.224	.309
Corrected coefficient of determination	.220	.218	.265	.204	.070	.098	.096	.210
F-Ratio	20.4	29.7	2.92	2.69	4.25	5.42	1.76	3.13
Significance level of F-Ratio	<.001	<.001	<.001	<.001	<.001	<.001	.080	<.001

[a]SMSA, noncentral city is the missing category.

[b]Miscellaneous services in the omitted category.

[c]No observations; coefficient could not be estimated.

[d]Average for age is the omitted category.

78

2. An instrumental variable technique has also been used to estimate PINC (permanent income) and NTRANS (negative transitory income) for persons in the MAS data.[25]

3. The residency variables are differently defined and differently labeled in CHAS and MAS. In CHAS, RES1 equals one for those living in the central city of an SMSA and RES2 equals one for those not living in an SMSA; SMSA, noncentral city is the omitted category. In MAS, "SMSA" is set equal to one for those living in an SMSA and equal to zero for those not living in an SMSA.

4. An indicator of spouse employment status, SPOUSE EMPSTAT, is included in the MAS equation for the unemployed; it equals one for those with a working wife. This variable is included as an ad hoc adjustment for the availability of group health insurance from the wife's employer.

5. Two indicators of self-reported health status, HSTAT1 and HSTAT2, are included in the MAS equations. HSTAT1 equals one if the respondent said that his health is better than average for persons the same age and HSTAT2 equals one if he said his health is worse; the omitted category is "health about the same." All else equal, persons in poor health and having a greater expectation of health care expenditure are predicted to have a greater demand for health insurance. (Other variables in Table 4–4 are defined in Table 4–1.)

Each of the four "group" equations in Table 4–4 is significant at the .001 level or better—that is, the hypothesis of no relationship between the dependent variable and the independent variable list can be rejected. The coefficients of determination from CHAS are nearly the same as from PPHI (see the previous section); however, the coefficient of determination is somewhat lower for the MAS unemployed equation, possibly due to instrumental variable (IV) estimation of PINC and NTRANS.

Only three variables were significant at the .10 level or better in each of the two unemployed equations, compared to eight significant variables in the OLS-estimated PPHI equation. This reduction in the number of significant variables probably reflects the smaller number of unemployed in CHAS and MAS—especially given the eight-variable categorization of industry. The sample size of the unemployed is 102 in CHAS, 146 in MAS, but 260 in PPHI.

With only a few exceptions, the parameter estimates from the CHAS and MAS group equations are remarkably similar, both qualitatively and quantitatively, to those from PPHI. All four CHAS and MAS coefficients estimated for PINC (permanent income) are positive and significantly different from zero; the PINC coefficients also are not significantly different from the PPHI estimates; in fact, the MAS estimates are very similar to the PPHI results, despite the use of an IV procedure for estimating PINC in MAS. Furthermore, the NTRANS (negative transitory income) coefficient estimated for the unemployed in MAS is significant at a high level and is virtually identical to the PPHI estimate. (The IV procedure used for estimating PINC in MAS also yields an estimate of NTRANS for the employed. We included it in the employed equation and obtained a similarly signed and similarly significant coefficient, although it is somewhat lower in absolute value, as is the estimate for PINC.) The coefficient estimated for NTRANS from CHAS is negative but not significant. The lack of significance may reflect our inability to measure the actual duration of unemployment from CHAS with certainty, and therefore to estimate the value of NTRANS correctly (see note 2, Chapter 3).

As economic theory predicts, the IV-estimated PRICE variable obtains negative coefficients in all four group equations. However, the coefficients are significant only in the two employed equations, which have a greater number of observations. Nevertheless, three of the four estimates are very similar in magnitude. (These results are not directly comparable to PPHI results, where group size categories were themselves used as proxies for price.)

The coefficients estimated for the noneconomic or more demographic variables in the CHAS and MAS group equations can be examined more briefly. Both CHAS and MAS yield significant and similar positive coefficients for the EDUC (education) variable in the group-employed equations, and the estimates are about twice as large as the nearly significant coefficient from PPHI. The effect of education on health insurance demands of the unemployed is less clear. The MAS estimate is negative but insignificant; the CHAS estimate is negative and significant; and the PPHI estimate is positive but not significant.

Unlike the somewhat discrepant finding from PPHI, Table 4–4 indicates that the age coefficients are significant and positive in three of the four group equations, as had been predicted. The age coefficient is negative but insignificant in the MAS unemployed equation.

The MAS and CHAS findings for the RACE (nonwhite) variable are consistent with the somewhat peculiar finding from PPHI. Both data sources reveal that the coefficient is negative for the employed, as predicted, but that it is positive for the unemployed. Furthermore, the MAS unemployed coefficient is significant.

The MAS and CHAS results for the SEX (female) variable are much the same as those from PPHI; all parameter estimates are negative and not significant. However, MAS and CHAS yield somewhat stronger results for the NCHILD (number of children) variable. The estimated coefficient is negative and significant, or nearly significant, in three of four cases. It is positive but highly insignificant in the MAS unemployed equation. Such findings may signal that the greater immediate financial "need" of a larger family supersedes the greater risk attached to not being insured.

The findings with respect to location of residence are somewhat puzzling. PPHI indicates that persons in urban areas have a greater demand for health insurance, while MAS indicates that persons in SMSAs have lower demands. This may be explained by the results from CHAS which, though not significant, indicate that demand is lower both in non-SMSA areas and in the central cities of SMSAs, SMSA-noncentral city being the omitted category. Thus, it is not surprising that MAS, which oversampled inner-city persons, obtained a negative coefficient on the SMSA variable. The CHAS and MAS results for MSTATUS (married) are not too dissimilar from the PPHI estimates; only the negative but insignificant coefficient for the unemployed in CHAS is different.

Again, some of the industry (IND1–IND8) variables are significant, especially in the employed equations, which further supports our conclusion from PPHI that access to health insurance depends substantially on the industry in which a person is employed. However, the magnitudes and significance levels of the coefficients estimated from CHAS and MAS are sometimes different from the results in PPHI. These differences may either reflect structural changes, or, more likely, may reflect the limitations of small and moderate samples in giving reliable parameter estimates for the entire country. The estimates from PPHI and MAS are the most similar, although the relative position of those in the miscellaneous services industry (the omitted category) has improved in the more recent MAS.

The CHAS and MAS coefficient estimates for the CLASS (self-employed) variable are similar to those from PPHI. The results from CHAS and MAS with respect to the COST (regional cost index) variable are more encouraging than those from PPHI. As predicted, we estimate positive coefficients for this variable in all four equations, although the estimate is significant at a high level in only one. The results are sufficient to warrant further investigation of our hypothesis that the demand for health insurance is related to regional variations in the cost of health care.

Several "new" variables are included in the MAS equations. The coefficient of the SPOUSE EMPSTAT variable indicates that a working wife increases the probability that a household with unemployed head will have health insurance by 9 percentage points, presumably because of the greater availability of group health insurance through the wife's employment. Although this magnitude is quantitatively important, it is not statistically significant. We also find that, contrary to expectations, "worse health" (HSTAT2) is associated with a 10 percentage point lower probability of having health insurance for the employed and a 9 percentage point lower probability for the unemployed, although only the former estimate is significant.

These findings may reflect institutional barriers to the acquisition of health insurance by those in "poor" health—so-called uninsurables or high-risk persons. That is, a health insurance market for this population may not exist. However, as predicted, employed persons reporting "better" health (HSTAT1) have a somewhat smaller demand for health insurance, although the coefficient is not significant. The HSTAT1 coefficient estimated for the unemployed is positive but highly insignificant.

As in the PPHI analysis, we must also ask how well the estimated relationships account for the loss of health insurance by the unemployed. If negative transitory income (NTRANS) is set equal to zero in the CHAS and MAS group equations, we estimate that the probability of having group health insurance rises by 1.5 and 7.0 percentage points, respectively. (The OLD model from PPHI estimates a 6.4 percentage point increase; the Probit model estimates 7.5 percentage points.) The CHAS figure is less than 5 percent of the estimated 1970 health insurance loss and the MAS figure is 20 to 25 percent of the estimated 1974–75 health insurance loss (see Table 3–1). These results support our conclusion from PPHI that only a small fraction of health insurance loss by the unemployed can be explained by income loss due to unemployment.

The Demands for Nongroup Health Insurance

In examining the four "nongroup" equations shown in the last four columns of Table 4–4, recall that individual or nongroup health insurance is likely to be purchased only if one does not have access to group health insurance. That is, the market for nongroup health insurance is "residual." Thus, we predict that health insurance demands can also be estimated from the nongroup insurance of those without group health insurance. In principle, the demand relationships estimated in this way should be the same as the group health insurance demand equations reported above. To test this hypothesis, and also to better understand the market for nongroup health insurance, we have estimated the "nongroup" relationships from CHAS and MAS. (PPHI did not have information on nongroup health insurance.)

The model is much the same as that used for estimating the "group" equations except that we have no index of price variation (PRICE), and the employment variables (IND1–IND8 and CLASS) are excluded for lack of theoretic justification in analysis of this nonemployment related market for health insurance.

Each of these four nongroup equations is significant at the .01 level or better. However, the coefficients of determination from MAS are somewhat higher than those from CHAS. In addition, more variables are significant at the .01 level or better in the MAS equations. Six of the 12 variables in the MAS employed equation are significant while only 2 of the 10 in the CHAS employed equation are significant. Similarly, 5 of the 12 variables in the MAS unemployed equation are significant while only 3 of the 11 variables in the CHAS unemployed equation are significant.

Despite several notable exceptions, the parameter estimates from the MAS nongroup equations are qualitatively and quantitatively similar to those obtained from the MAS group equations, or at least are not significantly different. For example, the PINC and NTRANS nongroup coefficients, both employed and unemployed, are very similar to their respective group coefficients. However, unlike the group equations, the MAS nongroup employed equation obtains positive and significant, or nearly significant, coefficients for the RACE (nonwhite) and SEX (female) variables. These findings may signal discrimination in the market for group health insurance—namely, that employed nonwhites and females do not have the same access to group health insurance as whites and males. Of course, the findings may also be spurious. (The 1970 CHAS obtains a negative and significant coefficient for the RACE variable in the employed equation.)

The CHAS nongroup coefficients are not so similar to their respective group coefficients as we found from MAS. In particular, contrary to both expectations and our findings from the group estimation, the CHAS nongroup unemployed equation estimates a positive coefficient for the NTRANS (negative transitory income) variable. Furthermore, the CHAS coefficient is both "large" quantitatively and significantly different from zero. Setting NTRANS equal to zero, we estimate that the probability of having individual health insurance is increased by 6.0 percentage points during unemployment. Although this finding may be viewed as evidence against our model, we believe that it can also be understood within the context of the model. Some unemployed persons who have lost group health insurance nevertheless have effective demands for health insurance that are met by purchase of individual or nongroup health insurance. That is, some nongroup health insurance is substituted for group health insurance lost due to unemployment. Although conversion of group health insurance to a nongroup policy is sometimes possible, acquiring nongroup health insurance is often not so easy. Like all large and infrequent purchases, it involves significant transaction expense, notably the time to make inquiries about independent health insurance plans, evaluate the alternatives, and make application for them. Thus, the extent of nongroup health insurance may increase with duration of unemployment. Furthermore, we might reasonably predict that it will increase the most for those with the greatest permanent incomes. If so, we predict a positive sign for the interaction between permanent income and duration of unemployment.

Unfortunately, the definition of this variable, proxying transaction costs in the substitution of nongroup health insurance, is very similar and highly colinear to our CHAS proxy for transitory income, essentially permanent wage income times the duration of unemployment. For this reason, we believe that estimation of a positive coefficient for the transitory income variable is spurious, reflecting not so much the transitory income effect as the delay in acquisition of nongroup health insurance by those with effective demand. Disentangling these separate effects was prevented by the severe colinearity, compounded by small sample size. (The MAS nongroup equation obtains a negative and significant coefficient for the NTRANS variable, as predicted. Apparently, the instrumental variable procedure used for estimating NTRANS in MAS does not suffer the same problem.)

Differences in the Quality of Health Insurance Demanded

The health insurance demands have been estimated above as if the choice set were dichotomous. We have modeled whether or not someone has health insurance but have not distinguished differences in its "quality" or comprehensiveness. The 1970 CHAS data were used to analyze such differences. The health insurance premium amount—call it PREM—is reported from CHAS for health insurance policies that were verified by insurers. We have divided PREM by our health insurance price index, PRICE, to obtain an estimate—called BENEFIT—for the expected value of benefits. We regard this as an index of health insurance quality. We have regressed this BENEFIT variable on essentially the same list of independent variables used in the group equations, except that a new variable has been added. The sample size for the unemployed ($N = 28$) was too small to estimate separate relationships by employment status, as done above. Instead, the unemployed and the employed were both included in the same relationship and a new variable UNEM—equal to one for the unemployed and zero for the employed—was introduced to isolate the effect of unemployment on health insurance quality. The results are as follows ($N = 813$):

BENEFIT = 303 + .00136*PINC   −   20.0*UNEM − 170*PRICE
(significance level)   (.086)   (.351)   (.000)

+ 2.54*EDUC − .0115*AGE + 7.66*RACE
   (.066)   (.975)   (.484)

+ 15.6*SEX + 4.54*NCHILD − 12.2*RES1
   (.367)   (.056)   (.238)

− 37.6*RES2 + 95.7*MSTAT + 39.4*IND1
   (.000)   (.000)   (.047)

+ 123*IND2 + 1.01*IND3 + 24.0*IND4
   (.026)   (.957)   (.044)

+ .409*IND5 − 6.35*IND6 − 30.0*IND7
   (.981)   (.644)   (.127)

+ 37.4*IND8 + 31.4*CLASS + .121*COST
   (.011)   (.029)   (.250)

Coefficient of determination	.375
Corrected coefficient of determination	.358
F-ratio	22.6
Significance of F-ratio	.000

Equation 4–8 does quite well statistically. It explains a substantial fraction of the variation, and 11 of the 21 independent variables are significant at the .10 level or better. However, the coefficient estimated for the employment status variable, UNEM, is not significant. Nevertheless, the coefficient estimate is negative and implies that the expected value of

health insurance is about 10 percent less for the unemployed than for otherwise similar employed persons. This is consistent with our conclusion from Chapter 3 that the health insurance held by the unemployed is somewhat lower in quality than that of the employed but that the differences are not dramatic.

To comment on the other coefficients in equation 4–8: The PINC and PRICE coefficients have the usual signs and are significant (the implicit price elasticity is − .980). Furthermore, the EDUC coefficient is significant and positive, as expected. Perhaps the most surprising aspect of the relationship is the apparent lack of association between the dependent variable and AGE. We cannot explain this finding. RACE and SEX are also not significant. Although NCHILD and MSTATUS are both positive and significant, as might be expected, it is not clear whether benefits increase more or less proportionately with the number of subscribers. (Of course, the insurers may also not discriminate such differences, in which case the premium may not reliably reflect the expected value of benefits; for example, the premium on a family policy is often not dependent on family size.) The RES1 and RES2 coefficients have the same signs as estimated above from CHAS.

Four of the eight industry variables (IND1–IND8) are significant. This supports our earlier conclusion that the provision of health insurance in this country depends importantly upon industry of employment. Except for IND1 and IND7, the signs and significance levels for these variables are not much different from those obtained in the CHAS group equations. The significant, negative coefficient for IND7 may reflect price discounts available to those employed in insurance companies. The positive and significant coefficient for CLASS is somewhat unexpected. The coefficient of COST is positive, as expected, but is not significant.

Health Insurance and the Demand
for Health Care by the Unemployed—A Digression

Although this study is primarily concerned with the impact of unemployment on the demand for health insurance, we digress briefly to explore the impact of health insurance on the demand for health care by the unemployed. It has been assumed throughout this book that health insurance increases health care expenditure, as many studies have shown to be true in the aggregate. We now test it for the unemployed. We use the health care expenditure estimates from the 1970 CHAS. To give a reasonably general yet easily understood relationship, we have included both the employed and the unemployed in the same model. Total family health care expenditure (EXP) has been somewhat arbitrarily regressed on the same variables included in the health insurance demand equations, except that the industry variables (IND1–IND8 and CLASS) have been excluded and two new variables have been introduced.[26] The first, INS1, equals one for anyone with health insurance and equals zero for anyone without it. The second new variable, INS2, is an interaction term and equals one for anyone who is unemployed and has health insurance and equals zero if one is either employed or unemployed and does not have health insurance. Unemployed persons are also identified in the equation, albeit discontinuously, by the NTRANS variable.[27] The estimated equation is as follows ($N = 1519$):

$$EXP = -797 + .0127*PINC - .0247*NTRANS + 20.56*EDUC$$

(significance level) (.041) (.509) (.099)

$$+ 8.44*AGE - 106*RACE + 45.0*SEX + 70.7*NCHILD$$

(.009) (.265) (.767) (.001)

$$- 71.4*RES1 - 217*RES2 + 339*MSTATUS$$

(.458) (.027) (.011)

$$+ 1.99*COST - 83.8*INS1 + 485*INS2$$

(.034) (.350) (.107)

Coefficient of determination	.045
Corrected coefficient of determination	.036
F-ratio	5.42
Significance Level of F-ratio	.000

Although the relationship does not explain a large fraction of the variance, 8 of the 11 independent variables are significant or nearly significant. Of course, the overall relationship is also significant.

The results for the health insurance variables (INS1 and INS2) are quite surprising. Contrary to empirical tradition, the INS1 variable indicates that health insurance does not lead to increased use of health care services by the general working population. In fact, it is estimated to lead to an $84 reduction, albeit nonsignificant, in family health care expense (the mean expense was $606). However, health insurance is estimated from the INS2 variable to increase annual health care expense by $485 in households where the head is unemployed. Furthermore, the coefficient estimate is very nearly significant at the usual .10 criterion.

Although it is premature to draw conclusions until alternative explanations can be investigated and the analysis can be replicated from other sources, these results have several interesting implications. First, the "moral hazard" of health insurance does not appear to influence the health care demands of the larger working population. Apparently, families with the head employed have sufficient income to purchase the desired level of health services and health insurance does not bias toward overuse. Previous findings suggesting such overutilization may reflect failure to control for employment status. Second, the finding that health insurance is important for the unemployed tends to indicate that inability to borrow against future income—a financial market failure—is the cause of reduced health care expenditures by the unemployed without health insurance and that such reduction is inefficient. Although this inference remains substantially speculative at this stage, nevertheless we believe that our findings demand a reexamination of the now-conventional wisdom that health insurance leads to overutilization of health services. Our results are more nearly consistent with the view that it corrects underutilization.

Examine now some other results from equation 4–9. Although the coefficient for NTRANS (negative transitory income) is not significant, it is almost twice as large in absolute value as the coefficient for the PINC (permanent income). Because the life-cycle theory of consumption predicts a smaller coefficient for transitory income than for permanent income, this result is also consistent with the hypothesis that financial market failure has led to inefficient underutilization of health services by the unemployed. The other parameter estimates conform to the usual expectations. Total health care expenditures are larger in households where the head is more educated, older, or female and in households with more children or living in areas with historically higher levels of utilization; health care expense is smaller for nonwhite households and for households living in central cities or living outside an SMSA, compared to living in a noncentral city of an SMSA.

A SIMULATION OF CYCLICAL VARIATION IN HEALTH INSURANCE LOSS

Congressional and other concerns about the health insurance loss associated with unemployment first emerged in the context of the 1974–75 recession. Furthermore, most of the legislative initiatives to extend health insurance to the unemployed (see Chapter 5) would have done so only during the immediate recessionary period. That is, health insurance loss was perceived as being merely a cyclical problem. In fact, the loss of health insurance due to unemployment is a persistent problem, albeit at a lower level, even during economic well-being. In this section we use the results of analyzing the 1975–76 MAS, our most recent data source, to simulate cyclical variation in the extent of health insurance lost due to unemployment. We do this to dramatize that such health insurance loss is an ongoing problem, as well as to demonstrate the degree of cyclical sensitivity.

Historical data on the probability and duration of unemployment— 1963 to 1975, and the individual months of 1974 and 1975—are used in Table 4–5 to simulate variation in the extent of health insurance loss due to unemployment. To abstract from secular growth in the level of income we have assumed that income is fixed at the level found in our 1975–76 data.[28] The group and nongroup MAS equations in Table 4–4 have been used to project the probabilities that the unemployed would have health insurance given actual unemployment experience in each of the periods indicated and to project the probability of their having had health insurance while employed.[29] The results are shown in the first two columns of Table 4–5.[30] Taking the difference between these results, we obtain estimates in column 3 for the percentage of unemployed heads who would have lost health insurance. The actual unemployment rates for household heads during the periods indicated are shown in column 4. In column 5 these unemployment rates are multiplied by the results in column 3 to obtain estimates for the percentage of households in the population at large—with or without unemployed head—losing health insurance because of unemployment.

First, the results indicate that our model does not suggest major variation in the unemployed worker's likelihood of losing health insurance over the business cycle. Whereas the unemployment rate in column 4 varies threefold from 1.9 percent to 5.8 percent for the 1963–75 interval, the percentage of unemployed heads losing health insurance only varies from 24.7 percent to 28.5 percent. Thus, the variation in column 5 arises largely because of variation in the unemployment rate. We have estimated in column 5 that the percentage of households losing health insurance would have ranged from 0.44 percent to 1.65 percent during the 1963–75 interval and would have been as high as 1.86 percent during the worst month of the 1974–75 recession. The results further suggest that that extent of health insurance loss during the 1974–75 recession was not much more than twice as large as it would have been during typical prerecessionary years.

Table 4-5 A Simulation of Health Insurance Loss from Historical Data on Unemployment

Period	Projected Health Insurance Coverage		(3) Estimated Percentage of Households with Unemployed Heads Losing Health Insurance $(1-2)$	(4) Unemployment Rate for Household Heads	(5) Estimated Percentage of All Households Losing Health Insurance (3×4)
	(1) Head Employed	(2) Head Unemployed			
1963	80.2%	51.7%	28.5%	3.7%	1.05%
1964	80.2%	52.2%	28.0%	3.3%	0.92%
1965	80.2%	53.1%	27.1%	2.8%	0.76%
1966	80.2%	54.0%	26.2%	2.2%	0.58%
1967	80.2%	55.0%	25.2%	2.1%	0.53%
1968	80.2%	55.2%	25.0%	1.9%	0.48%
1969	80.2%	55.5%	24.7%	1.8%	0.44%
1970	80.2%	55.0%	25.2%	2.9%	0.73%
1971	80.2%	53.4%	26.8%	3.7%	0.99%
1972	80.2%	53.0%	27.2%	3.3%	0.90%
1973	80.2%	54.3%	25.9%	2.9%	0.75%
1974	80.2%	54.5%	25.7%	3.3%	0.85%
1975	80.2%	51.7%	28.5%	5.8%	1.65%
1974					
January	80.2%	54.9%	25.3%	3.5%	0.88%
February	80.2%	54.5%	25.7%	3.6%	0.92%
March	80.2%	53.8%	26.4%	3.4%	0.90%

Table 4-5 *continued*

April	80.2%	53.5%	26.7%	3.1%	0.83%
May	80.2%	53.9%	26.3%	2.8%	0.74%
June	80.2%	55.1%	25.1%	2.9%	0.73%
July	80.2%	54.7%	25.5%	2.8%	0.71%
August	80.2%	54.5%	25.7%	3.0%	0.77%
September	80.2%	55.0%	25.2%	3.0%	0.76%
October	80.2%	54.6%	25.6%	3.2%	0.82%
November	80.2%	54.7%	25.5%	3.7%	0.94%
December	80.2%	54.1%	25.5%	4.5%	1.15%
1975					
January	80.2%	54.2%	26.0%	6.3%	1.64%
February	80.2%	53.1%	27.1%	6.6%	1.79%
March	80.2%	52.4%	27.8%	6.7%	1.86%
April	80.2%	51.3%	28.9%	6.2%	1.79%
May	80.2%	51.2%	29.0%	5.9%	1.71%
June	80.2%	51.9%	28.3%	5.8%	1.64%
July	80.2%	51.6%	28.6%	5.6%	1.60%
August	80.2%	51.0%	29.2%	5.2%	1.52%
September	80.2%	51.2%	29.0%	5.0%	1.45%
October	80.2%	51.2%	29.0%	5.1%	1.48%
November	80.2%	50.3%	29.9%	5.2%	1.55%
December	80.2%	49.9%	30.3%	5.6%	1.70%

Source: Column 4—*Handbook of Labor Statistics 1976*, p. 132; *1973*, p. 155. For columns 1–3 and 5, see text.

These findings, however, merely reflect the results of a simulation exercise. As seen in Chapter 3, the percentage of unemployed heads who actually lost health insurance during the early 1970s was considerably larger than estimated in Table 4-5. Even if historical income levels were used in the simulation, the results would not approximate actual experience in these years. The inability of our model—either the MAS model or the models estimated from PPHI and CHAS—to replicate such historical experience signals structural change. We believe that such structural instability of the model reflects a recent social innovation—namely, that unions are now beginning to negotiate continuation of group health insurance benefits during layoffs. Of course, misspecification of the model itself is a further possibility.

SUMMARY OF FINDINGS

In this chapter we have used multivariate procedures to analyze the loss of health insurance due to unemployment and to isolate those factors which, in addition to employment itself, influence the magnitude of health insurance coverage.

Since the theory of health insurance has received much attention in recent years we did not pursue a fully comprehensive discussion of the underlying theoretic model. Instead we gave special attention to several theoretic considerations that are especially relevant to this study. First, we indicated that previous analyses of the effect of income on the demand for health insurance do not generalize to the large and transitory income reductions associated with loss of employment; it was necessary to estimate a transitory income elasticity (or effect) for assessing the impact of job loss, and associated income loss, on the demand for health insurance. Second, we also suggested that continuation of group health insurance by the former employer is significant and that loss of group health insurance by the unemployed is not fully arbitrary or capricious but rather reflects underlying economic factors. That is, we suggested that unemployed workers continue to demand health insurance from their previous employer and that these unemployed worker demands partly determine the extent of continuation. Though this prospect seemed counterintuitive, it has become more credible given recent understanding of the importance of temporary layoffs in the theory of the firm.

Data from 1970, 1972 and 1975–76 were used to estimate group and nongroup health insurance demand relationships. In most cases the health insurance demands were estimated separately for the employed and the unemployed to allow for interaction between work status and the other independent variables. The estimation strongly supported our hypothesis that unemployed workers continue to demand group health insurance from their previous employer. In particular, continuation of group health insurance during unemployment was shown to be systematically (and significantly) related to the economic variables—income and price—as well as to the other demographic characteristics.

The quantitative importance of continuation is however another matter. Only a small fraction—between 5 and 25 percent—of actual health insurance loss by the unemployed can be explained by our modeling effort. After considering several alternative explanations, we conclude that many unemployed workers simply do not have the opportunity to continue group health insurance from their previous employer. Either the employer is insensitive to the demands for continuation of health insurance during unemployment, or the employed workers themselves are insensitive to the prospect of unemployment and fail to transmit their "true" demands by negotiating continuation of group health insurance during unemployment as part of the terms of employment. Thus, the level of health insurance among the unemployed may be inefficiently too low (or suboptimal), assuming that the employer's group price in fact represents the social cost of continuing the insurance. (This prospect is further discussed in Chapter 5.) That is, we attribute much of the unemployment-related reduction in health insurance to a health insurance market failure. The reduction seems to be largely an artifact of the predominant work-group institutional mechanism for financing health insurance in our country and may bear little or no relation to underlying demand and cost considerations.

An employed worker's likelihood of having health insurance also depends substantially on the industry of employment, even after controlling for demographic and other relevant characteristics of the worker. That is, the provision of health insurance to the employed also depends importantly on institutional arrangements unrelated to demand variation. In addition, a self-employed worker is much less likely to have group health insurance than an otherwise similar nonself-employed worker, and a female or nonwhite head of household is less likely to have group health insurance than an otherwise similar male or white head of household. We also found that, contrary to expectations, those with "poor" health are less likely to have health insurance than those with average health. This finding may reflect institutional barriers to the acquisition of health insurance by such so-called uninsurable or high-risk persons. That is, a health insurance market for this population may not exist.

We have estimated that the expected value of benefits from health insurance is about 10 percent less for the unemployed than for otherwise similar employed persons. This supports our conclusion from Chapter 3 that the "quality" of health insurance lost due to unemployment is not too much different from the average.

We have also briefly explored—as a digression—the impact of unemployment on the demand for health care. The results were surprising. Contrary to empirical tradition, we found that health insurance does not lead to an increased use of health care services by the general working population. However, we found that health insurance increases health care expenses by $485 per year in households where the head is unemployed. Although it is premature to draw conclusions until alternative explanations can be investigated and the analysis can be replicated from other sources, the results have a variety of interesting implications. First, the "moral hazard" associated with health insurance would not appear to influence the health care demands of the larger working population. Apparently, families with the head employed have sufficient income to purchase the desired level of health services and health insurance does not bias toward overuse. Previous findings suggesting the contrary may reflect failure to control for employment status. Second, the finding that health insurance is important for the unemployed tends to indicate that inability to borrow against future income—a financial market failure—is the cause of reduced health care expenditure by the unemployed without health insurance and that such reduction is inefficient. However, such inference remains substantially speculative at this stage. Nevertheless, we believe that our findings demand a reexamination of the now-conventional wisdom that health insurance leads to over utilization of health services. Our results are more nearly consistent with the view that it corrects underutilization.

Finally, we have used our analysis of the 1975–76 data to simulate cyclical variation in the extent of health insurance lost because of unemployment. Health insurance loss by the unemployed had been perceived as being merely a recessionary problem. However, the simulation demonstrates that the problem persists, albeit at a lower level, even in time of economic well-being. In particular, the results suggest that the extent of health insurance loss during the 1974–75 recession was no more than twice as large as it would be during typical nonrecessionary years.

NOTES

1. Assume that $0 \leq \gamma(I) \leq 1$ and that $\partial \gamma / \partial I < 0$; also assume $E(X) \bullet [1 - \gamma(I)] < P_1 I$.

2. Health care expense is not fully exogenous but also depends on the extent of health insurance coverage. See the extensive theoretic and empirical literature on "moral hazard"—e.g., Arrow (1963, 1971), Pauly (1968), Rosett and Huang (1973), and Newhouse and Phelps (1974).

3. See Phelps (1973, 1976); Arrow (1976); Nordquist and Wu (1976); and Goldstein and Pauly (1976).

4. E.g., see Friedman (1957) and Modigliani and Brumberg (1954).

5. In 1960 the average loading fee was 10 percent for group health insurance and 96 percent for individual health insurance (MacIntyre 1962).

6. It is not known how many more unemployed persons had the opportunity of continuing group health insurance but chose not to do so.

7. Many collective bargaining agreements now provide for continuation of health insurance coverage after layoff. For example, UAW SUB (supplemental unemployment benefits) plans include extension of employer-paid benefits.

8. Although the tax-free employer contribution is usually fixed, many employers now offer more than one health insurance plan—e.g., a "high option" and a "low option" plan. Even so, the freedom of choice is still more limited than it is in the private market.

9. We assume that the employer-paid part of the insurance premium could have been received as wages by the worker group in lieu of the insurance contribution. (Of course, individual workers do not have this alternative.)

   Goldstein and Pauly (1976) have used a Tiebout-type model to analyze the determination of group health insurance within a firm seeking to minimize its total labor cost. Their analysis finds that the equilibrium depends on the average marginal benefit of the health insurance. Under reasonable conditions—namely, linearity of the demand curve—the average marginal benefit is equal to the average worker's marginal benefit and the level of health insurance provided is also the mean quantity demanded, as assumed in the text.

Goldstein and Pauly also model the determination of group health insurance by a union, contending that Q_{group} is determined as the median quantity demanded inasmuch as the median voter nominally determines the outcome of majority voting. We believe that this analysis is less persuasive because vote trading is probable and will cause the result to approach the more optimal one discussed above.

10. Of course, the estimators would be more efficient—i.e., have lower variance—if Q_i^D were actually observable and could be used as the dependent variable.

11. Of course, with a contributory plan, an individual may elect not to participate in the group health insurance plan and thereby adjust discontinuously for overinsurance. However, given the extraordinary price advantage of group insurance it seems unlikely that someone would forego a group insurance package to purchase a smaller quantity of individual health insurance.

12. See Chapter 3 for discussion of this data source.

13. Although the self-administered PPHI questionnaire was designed to skip the unemployed in asking for the work-group size, some of the unemployed errored and answered the question in sufficient numbers to permit significant estimation, assigning mean values to those not reporting work-group size.

14. Mincer (1960) has also defined permanent and transitory income in this way.

15. See Phelps (1973), pp. 61–63.

16. E.g., see Grossman (1972).

17. Occupation variables were not found to be significant or quantitatively important to the model.

18. Various studies have shown substantial regional variation in health care costs and it has now become commonplace to include regional dummy variables to proxy such regional differences. We believe that our approach is more satisfactory inasmuch as it more directly represents the relevant differences.

19. The "unemployed" equations were estimated from PPHI using data on all unemployed household heads reporting health insurance status. In the interest of economy the "employed" equations were estimated using a 10 percent sample of all employed household heads reporting health insurance status. However, persons over the age of 65 were excluded from all analyses; to estimate WAGE it was necessary to select only those unemployed having some earnings, and therefore employment, in the previous year. Finally, persons employed at time of survey, but reporting

receipt of unemployment compensation during the previous year, were excluded from the analysis.

20. In the case of dichotomous variables, the OLS-estimated effects are the same as the coefficients.

21. Computed from weekly continuation rates in Kaitz (1970), Table 4, p. 13.

22. The outcome is somewhat different from OLS estimation. The typical unemployed worker is estimated to have a 28.1 percent probability of having health insurance during unemployment and to have had a 71.6 percent probability while employed. Setting NTRANS equal to zero implies that the probability while unemployed rises to 34.5 percent, a 6.4 percentage point increase. Thus, the OLS modeling implies that the loss of income due to unemployment explains $6.4/(71.6 - 28.1)$ or 14.7 percent of the total health insurance loss.

23. Even the at-risk analysis in Chapter 3, which identifies workers most likely to become unemployed, finds that the probability of health insurance coverage among workers at-risk of unemployment is only 14.1 percentage points lower than that of the worker population at large.

24. CHAS reports the group size for all persons with verification of health insurance; and Phelps (1973, p. 64) gives the estimated "loading fee" by group size. These data were combined to form the PRICE variable (see text); PRICE was regressed on industry and occupation variables as shown below ($N = 681$):

PRICE = 1.14   −   .0208*OCC1

(significance level)   (.074)

− .0116*OCC2   +   .0510*OCC3   + .0213*OCC4   −   .0511*IND1
    (.236)   (.719)   (.668)   (.235)

− .0165*IND2   −   .00558*IND3   − .0160*IND4   −   .0380*IND5
    (.705)   (.752)   (.161)   (.023)

+ .00774*IND6   −   .0157*IND7   − .0361*IND8
    (.578)   (.398)   (.009)

Coefficient of determination	.105
Corrected coefficient of determination	.032
F-ratio	1.87
Significance of F-ratio	.035

(Table A-1, Appendix A, identifies the industry and occupation variables.)
The industry and occupation of most recent employment were substituted

into this relationship to obtain instrumental variable estimates of the PRICE variable for all household heads in CHAS and MAS, including those without group health insurance.

25. Elsewhere, Frank Sloan has used MAS data on total family income and source of income, as well as the employment status of household head and spouse (if any), to estimate the household's permanent (full-time) wage and nonwage income. Transitory income is derived as a residual from the difference between actual income and the instrumental variables estimate of permanent income. We have used Sloan's estimates.

26. We also tried introducing the UNEMPLOYED variable used above but found it to be highly insignificant.

27. We were not able to control for health status.

28. Except for NTRANS the magnitudes of all other variables are also implicitly fixed since historical variation in their values did not change the results.

29. The employed (D_e) and unemployed (D_u) worker demands for health insurance were formed as a composite of the group (G) and nongroup (N) equations estimated in Table 4-4:

$$D_e = G_e + N_e \, (1 - G_e)$$
$$D_u = G_u + N_u \, (1 - G_u)$$

(Recall that nongroup equations were estimated only from the experience of those not having group health insurance.) Historical data were taken from the *Handbook of Labor Statistics 1976* and *1973*. NTRANS was defined as the average duration of unemployment times average weekly earnings.

30. Our estimate here for the percentage of unemployed workers having had health insurance while employed is very similar to the lower-bound at-risk estimate from MAS in Table 3-1—82.5 percent compared to 80.2 percent from Table 4-5.

5

The Public Policy Implications of Health Insurance for the Unemployed

The main analytic findings of this study have already been summarized in the conclusions of Chapters 3 and 4, as well as in Chapter 1. In this final chapter we examine these findings in the context of the public policy concerns surrounding the loss of health insurance by the unemployed. In particular, we wish to explore the implications of various alternatives for extending health insurance to the unemployed. We begin with a discussion of the various "emergency" health insurance programs proposed as federal legislation during the 1974–75 recession. Next we explore the general implications of this study for expansion of public health insurance to the unemployed as well as with respect to specific legislative proposals.

We suggest a nongovernmental solution in the third section of this chapter. In particular, we recommend the development of alternative institutional arrangements for making group health insurance available to the unemployed. Our data suggest that such social innovation would solve much or most of the problem health insurance loss by the unemployed. Finally, we briefly consider the implications of this study for national health insurance.

CONGRESSIONAL INITIATIVES TO EXTEND HEALTH INSURANCE TO THE UNEMPLOYED

As noted in Chapter 1, the 1974–75 recession prompted Congressional interest in extending public health insurance protection to the unemployed. Avram Yedida, a consultant to the Kaiser-Permanente health plan in California, first brought the problem to the attention of Congress in January 1975, when unemployment stood at 8.2 percent. Only one in four unemployed workers were thought to have health insurance, reflecting the strong institutional linkage in this country between health insurance and employment. By March 11, 1975 three major bills that would extend health insurance to the unemployed had been introduced in Congress.

S 496—Bentsen.   This bill introduced by Senator Lloyd Bentsen (D–Texas), would have extended Medicare–Part A hospitalization benefits to all unemployed persons eligible for unemployment compensation.[1] Benefits, deductible, and coinsurance features were to be the same as those applicable to other Part A beneficiaries. The program was to be administered by the Social Security Administration, as part of the existing Medicare–Part A program. Providers were to be reimbursed in accordance with existing Part A payment procedures and would be subject to Medicare's quality, health and safety, and utilization controls. The costs of this health insurance program, estimated by HEW to be $1.25 billion, were to be met from federal general revenue expenditures. The program was to last only one year.

S 625—Kennedy.   Senator Edward M. Kennedy (D–Massachusetts) introduced this bill which would have paid the premium to continue employment-related health insurance to any unemployed worker eligible for unemployment compensation and not covered or eligible for coverage from a spouse's or parent's policy. The Secretary of Labor was to arrange to pay the insurance carriers, employers, or health and welfare trusts for continuation of the unemployed worker's health insurance coverage, including a reasonable amount for administrative expense. State unemployment compensation agencies were to certify individuals as eligible for the health insurance benefits program and were to be reimbursed for their costs by the federal government. State agencies were to inform carriers, employers, or health and welfare trusts of the initial eligibility of the unemployed worker. State agencies were also to be responsible for paying the premiums. The program was to be financed from federal subsidies paid from general revenues. HEW estimated the cost at $1.54 billion in fiscal 1976, assuming an 8 percent unemployment rate. The bill was to become effective on enactment in early 1975 and to expire June 30, 1976.

HR 5000—Rostenkowski.[2] Representative Dan Rostenkowski (D–Illinois) advanced this proposal to require all group health insurance contracts to cover workers who lose their jobs and are entitled to unemployment compensation benefits. Coverage would last as long as the worker is eligible for unemployment compensation or a maximum of one year. Employers would have had 14 months to write the requirement into their group health contracts. Meanwhile, a temporary program would have required employers to restore or maintain health insurance protection for their unemployed workers. This temporary program was to be financed by a federal loan to be paid off from a 1 percent tax on all group health insurance plans. William C. Hsiao, an actuarial consultant, estimated that the bill would run between $2 billion and $2.5 billion per year, increasing the cost of group health insurance by 7 to 8 percent. Employers and employees were to pay this amount on the same shared basis as in the existing group plan.

Various alternative approaches for extending health insurance to the unemployed were also discussed. One of these would have made all unemployed persons and their families eligible for Medicaid.[3] Another proposal (S 970—Hartke) would have established a catastrophic health insurance program for the unemployed, providing hospital coverage after the fifteenth day and medical coverage after an outlay of $1,000. It was also suggested that health insurance be included as an unemployment benefit and that it be financed by an increase in the employment program tax.

At least three obstacles prevented timely enactment of health insurance for the unemployed. First, the Ford administration strongly opposed such legislation. Second, a major dispute arose over whether legislation should require employers to provide protection and rely on the private sector to finance and administer it, or whether the program should be federally financed and controlled. And, third, four Congressional committees held public hearings on the issue, each claiming jurisdiction and turning the debate into a struggle for political credit. The various initiatives subsequently died in committee as the 1974–75 recession ended and the economy rebounded. Health insurance for the unemployed was largely viewed as being an antirecession measure and the recession problem had been solved, albeit temporarily. Congress has made no subsequent indications of interest in health insurance for the unemployed.

EVALUATING THE EXTENSION
OF HEALTH INSURANCE TO THE UNEMPLOYED

In this section, we set out some of the criteria that should be used in evaluating the legislative proposals described in the previous section. Though we do not attempt a rigorous evaluation of each proposal, we will use our findings from the earlier chapters to formulate some of the policy implications they present. Even with the new information developed in this study, we do not have sufficient understanding of the problem to come to a definitive conclusion about any of these proposals. Nevertheless, we believe that our study offers new perspectives for evaluation and answers some of the questions that were unanswered when these proposals were first considered.

Again, the normative questions remain unanswered. We still do not know whether it is desirable to extend public health insurance to the unemployed or, if it is desirable, what the rationale for doing so is. Is health insurance for the unemployed sought because its advocates believe it will result in more efficient investment in human resources? Or is the motive something else such as equity in income distribution or a movement toward national health insurance? Though we cannot answer these questions, we will explore the implications for extending public health insurance to the unemployed *as if* such intervention is warranted.

Though we have not answered the normative questions, we were able to examine in some detail certain positive or descriptive issues, especially (1) the extent, kind, and distribution of health insurance lost by the unemployed; (2) how well Medicaid substitutes for loss of private health insurance; and (3) the behavioral determinants and consequences of health insurance loss. These issues concern what actually happens or, as a corollary, what might happen if various health insurance alternatives were enacted. We now consider some of the implications of our answers to these questions.

Magnitude of the Health Insurance Loss

First and perhaps most important, the magnitude of health insurance loss during the 1974–75 recession was seriously overestimated and therefore misrepresented to Congress. Data available at that time (for example, see Tables 2–2 and 2–3, and Kolodrubetz) suggested that fewer than one in four unemployed workers had health insurance and that roughly two in four unemployed workers had lost their health insurance due to unemployment.[4] Our more recent data indicate that 54 to 60 percent of unemployed household heads—the more relevant category—still had health insurance, either individual insurance or continued group insurance; 40 to 46 percent of unemployed heads did not have health insurance. We further estimate that only 20 to 35 percent of unemployed household heads lost their health insurance when they lost their jobs. That is, the magnitude of private health insurance loss during the 1974–75 recession was at least a third less than had been assumed in discussions of the proposals to extend "emergency" health insurance to the unemployed, or, equivalently, the extent of health insurance lost was thought to be 50 percent greater than it actually was. This error was a result of two factors. First, over the past five years there has been a dramatic 20 percentage point (or more) increase in the rate of group health insurance continuation to the unemployed (see Table 3–1). This probably reflects a trend toward negotiating such benefits as part of the fringe benefit package. Second, unemployed persons who have lost their group health insurance seem to be substituting individual insurance at about a 5 percentage point higher rate.

In addition, we have found that Medicaid and other public sources of health care jointly constitute a significant program of public health insurance for the unemployed and therefore may substantially mitigate the consequences of private health insurance loss. Between 19 and 31 percent of the unemployed without private health insurance receive health care from Medicaid and similar sources. Another 10 to 18 percent receive at least some health care from sources like V.A. and workmen's compensation. This leaves between 20 and 33 percent of the unemployed with neither private health insurance nor public health insurance alternatives. Unfortunately, we do not know how many people in each of these categories had health insurance while they were employed, so we cannot estimate the actual *loss* of such insurance. Nevertheless, it seems reasonable to assume that at least some unemployed persons who are receiving public assistance with health care costs did have private health insurance while employed. Thus, the percentage of unemployed workers losing health insurance-type protection altogether (private or public) is even less than the 20 to 35 percent indicated above.

Of course, we cannot predict how Congress would have responded to our lower estimate for the magnitude of the problem. Nevertheless, it seems likely that Congress would have given even less attention than it did to the "emergency" health insurance proposals because the benefits of such proposals would have been lower.

Efficiency Considerations

Our estimate of health insurance loss, however, does not reliably indicate the cost of providing health insurance to the unemployed. If public health insurance was made available to the unemployed—either to all unemployed or only to recipients of unemployment compensation—we predict that the magnitude of private health insurance loss resulting from unemployment would increase and approach the limit where all unemployed workers eligible for the program lose their health insurance. As long as public health insurance is a satisfactory substitute, the worker's cost of continuing private health insurance during unemployment can be saved without any loss of health insurance protection. Thus, present arrangements for continuing of group health insurance during unemployment would be allowed to expire; individual insurance would not be continued or purchased on loss of employment; and group insurance would not be obtained from a working spouse or from parents.[5]

In other words, the loss of health insurance by the unemployed is not exogenous; it is not possible to "target" benefits only to those who otherwise would have lost their health insurance. Some portion of the benefits will spill over to those who would not have lost their health insurance, and the magnitude of this unproductive spill-over increases as the magnitude of the real problem decreases—that is, the benefit-cost ratio decreases. Our reduced estimate for the magnitude of the problem of health insurance loss by the unemployed implies that a program of public health insurance for the unemployed would be less efficient in whatever sense is relevant, unless movement toward national health insurance is the ultimate objective.

The Rostenkowski proposal would not have been subject to this spill-over problem. His resolution (HR 5000) was to require that all group health insurance contracts include "costless" continuation of health insurance benefits to unemployed workers. The plan was to be financed by an increase in the price employed workers paid for group health insurance. This seemingly ingenious "private" plan would keep the cost of financing health insurance for the unemployed out of the federal budget altogether. However, it too has a hidden cost: it would create a serious distortion in the market for health insurance that could result in less health insurance overall. It had been estimated that HR 5000 would increase the cost of group health insurance by 7 to 8 percent, although a somewhat lower estimate is now appropriate in light of our finding that the magnitude of health insurance loss had been over-estimated.

Even if the cost increased by only 5 percent, our estimate for the effect of price on the demand for group health insurance implies that the prevalence of such health insurance would decrease by over 15 percentage points.[6] However, this ignores the fact that the increase in cost is not a "pure" price increase but that additional benefits—from continuation of health insurance—would be obtained by some but not all workers. Even so, we assume that the benefits are valued at less than cost or they would already have been obtained. Of course, those not at-risk of unemployment would not value the additional benefits at all. Thus, the actual reduction in the demand for group health insurance may be considerably less than 15 percentage points. However, the reduction could also be considerably larger for those firms that experience a greater than average incidence of unemployment among their workers and therefore require a greater than average health insurance premium increase to finance continuation during unemployment. In sum, it is just possible that more health insurance would be lost by the employed than is gained by the unemployed. The existence of such hidden costs of legislation underscores the importance of policy analysis in guiding the development of effective public policy.

A further effect of any governmental plan to extend health insurance to the unemployed would be an increase in the unemployment rate. Conceptually, any program of benefits to the unemployed reduces the cost of being unemployed; it makes it more attractive to leave a job and, once unemployed, less attractive to take another job. Empirical studies of unemployment, including our own in Appendix A, have in fact found that the extent of unemployment varies importantly with the generosity of unemployment benefits.[7] Using our estimates in Appendix A and assuming that a family health insurance policy costs $40 per month, we calculate that the annual probability of unemployment would be increased by 1 percentage point and the mean duration of unemployment would be increased by one-quarter week if health insurance were provided to all those eligible for unemployment compensation. However, as Stephen Marston (1975, p. 14) suggests, the normative implications of such a result are not clear; although most persons tend to assume that unemployment is undesirable, it is also possible that the benefits from prolonged job search (for example, having time to find a higher paying job) exceed the more obvious costs. Nevertheless, we should be aware that any governmental program of health insurance for the unemployed—even Rostenkowski's—has such implications for job search and the unemployment rate.

Equity Issues

HEW Secretary Caspar W. Weinberger raised several issues about equity in testifying on two proposals to extend health insurance to the unemployed. Regarding S 496 he said (p. 36):

> *The point to be emphasized, Mr. Chairman, is that the eligibility criteria for current Medicare beneficiaries are different and generally more restrictive than would be the case for the unemployed. It would be difficult to explain to a disabled person why he had to wait two years for Medicare benefits and why, even then, his children would not be eligible, when healthy unemployed persons and their dependents would have no waiting period.*

> *The equity issue comes even more strongly into focus when you consider that persons aged 65 and over who are not insured for Part A of Medicare may obtain such coverage only by paying a premium, which is now $36 per month and will increase to $40 per month in July. S 496 would provide identical coverage for the unemployed at no cost.*

When it came to S 625 Weinberger asked (p. 36):

> *Would it be fair to the person eligible under a $25 per month health plan for the Federal government to continue that premium when another person eligible under an $85 per month health plan also had his full premium paid? Would it be fair to the working taxpayers of this country, millions of whom have little or no health coverage, to use their taxes to continue paying a premium of $85 per month for some of the unemployed?*

There are other questions of equity as well. Should we—as proposed in S 496—also extend health insurance to the unemployed who did not have health insurance while employed? Why not also extend it to the unemployed not eligible for unemployment compensation? This study has very little to say about the answers to such questions. We merely suggest that equity and efficiency cannot be discussed in isolation; they are interrelated. Whether or not it is fair to give $25 to one and $85 to another depends on the rationale for intervention. If the purpose is to support efficient investment in health-type human resources, it may or may not be equitable; but if the purpose is to move toward national health insurance, it is clearly not equitable—at least not in the short run—because national health insurance implies equal benefits. In any event, a program of health insurance benefits for the unemployed is broadly compatible with the usual criteria for income distributional equity. As pointed out in Chapter 3, the probability of health insurance loss resulting from unemployment is highest for young workers, non-white workers, unmarried workers, female workers, workers with large families, and workers with low incomes. We further see that the unemployed not having health insurance while employed are an even less privileged class.

Administrative Efficiency

Administrative efficiency is another issue raised by Secretary Weinberger. He testified at length about the difficulties and costs of administering S 496 and S 625. For example:

Since S 625 would extend the coverage the individual had while working a mechanism would have to be established to verify eligibility through a previously existing health insurance contract and to pay premiums to the appropriate carrier.

Thousands of employers and health and welfare trust funds across the country would have to certify as to terminated employee's eligibility under a pre-existing health plan. Many of these employers and trust funds will be unable, or unwilling, to provide this certification or will not understand the necessity of performing this function. There would be tremendous administrative problems involved in education and enforcement to ensure that these provisions are carried out. . . .

And what of the State employment offices that must then pay the premium to keep the health insurance in force? What is their administrative capability to pay millions of dollars of premiums in varying amounts to thousands of health and welfare trusts, employers, or carriers? (p. 35)

Although administrative costs are correctly included in the evaluation of any public program, they are especially important in this case because unemployment—and therefore the resulting loss of health insurance—is a transitional problem. Both S 496 and S 625, for example, would involve rapid turnover of enrollees with a disproportionate share of program resources going toward determination of eligibility, records handling, and other enrollment-disenrollment costs. However, the private-insurance alternative HR 5000 avoids such transactional expense by avoiding the necessity of changing from one health insurance plan (or means of financing it) to another. (Of course, we have seen that HR 5000 has another flaw.) The Medicaid alternative also avoids many of these costs because only those unemployed persons with actual medical expense would participate in the program. Furthermore, as shown in Chapter 3, Medicaid already provides benefits to many unemployed (in conjunction with the AFDC Unemployed Father program) and thus is experienced in administering health insurance benefits for the unemployed.

Cost Control

Our final evaluative consideration is cost control. Private health insurance has various features—for example, coinsurance and deductibles—designed to discourage overutilization of health care services. It is not clear whether such mechanisms are effective, or, if they are effective, whether the resulting reductions in health care expense are desirable. Nevertheless, it may be more efficient to conserve in this way on health care expenditures than not to provide health insurance benefits to the unemployed at all. To the extent that budgetary considerations are important, Medicaid, which has neither coinsurance nor deductibles, may not be an efficient alternative. (In addition, Medicaid may have a serious equity problem because benefits vary substantially from state to state.) A program of public health insurance for the unemployed with effective cost control features might even lead to reducing public expenditures for health care of the unemployed currently eligible for Medicaid.

INCREASING ACCESS OF THE UNEMPLOYED
TO PRIVATE HEALTH INSURANCE—A PROPOSAL

Health insurance is "lost" during unemployment for two somewhat independent reasons:

1. The loss of income associated with unemployment implies a reduction in the demand for health insurance, portrayed in Figure 5-1 as a downward shift in the demand curve.

2. Because group health insurance costs about half as much as equivalent individual insurance, and because almost all group health insurance is purchased through an employer, loss of employment typically entails loss of this group price advantage, portrayed as a shift in the supply curve from S_{group} to $S_{\text{individual}}$ in Figure 5-1.

Thus the total reduction in health insurance resulting from unemployment, $Q_E - Q_U''$, can be separated into income and price effects. The quantity $Q_E - Q_U'$ measures the reduction in health insurance due to the decrease in income and the quantity $Q_U' - Q_U''$ measures the reduction due to the increase in price.

Using several different sources of data, in Chapter 4 we sought to estimate the income effect and found that it could explain no more than 5 to 25 percent of the unemployed's actual loss of health insurance. After considering several alternative explanations, we concluded that only the price effect could explain a very substantial part of the remaining loss. That is, we believe that the price effect accounts for most of the residual—approaching 75 to 95 percent of the health insurance that is lost during unemployment. Furthermore, we now suggest that this price-induced reduction in health insurance is inefficient. We recommend a

Figure 5-1
The Income and Price Effects and the Potential Welfare Gain

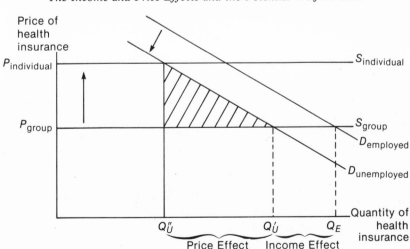

nongovernmental alternative for avoiding it and thereby solving much or most of the health insurance loss problem.

The economies of scale and substantially lower prices associated with group or collective purchase of health insurance imply that health insurance is a collective-consumption good and therefore that the private market may not provide it in optimal quantities. Though the workplace provides a private market setting in which the pecuniary externality is internalized for most workers, no comparable mechanism for internalizing the externality is generally available to most of the unemployed. The market fails to provide an institutional alternative for that purpose. Thus, most of the reduction in health insurance caused by unemployment is believed to reflect shortcomings in the predominant work-group institutional mechanism for financing health insurance in this country. Furthermore, we now speculate that this problem can be solved by one or more institutional innovations that involve neither governmental provision nor governmental financing of health insurance for the unemployed.

First of all, we suggest that the externality can continue to be internalized within the workplace. In particular, we suggest that insurers and employers *permit* continuation of group health insurance from a former employer so long as the unemployed worker pays its true social cost. (Recall that HR 5000 would *compel* continuation of group health insurance; S 625 would have the government finance such continuation; and S 496 would provide Medicare benefits as a substitute for private health insurance which is lost.) This cost includes the full health insurance premium amount paid by the employer to the insurer (including any portion formerly paid by the employer) plus any costs borne by the employer in continuing the health insurance—for example, the costs of collecting the premium and providing assistance with claims.[8] If continuation were offered on this basis, neither the employer nor the insurer would be worse off and yet the unemployed workers who could purchase health insurance at something approaching the group rate—assuming that the employer costs are minimal—would be better off.[9] The quantity of health insurance purchased by the unemployed would increase from Q_U'' to Q_U' in Figure 5-1, and the gain in social welfare or efficiency would be measured by the cross-hatched triangular area.

Although employers and insurers would have no reason not to offer continuation of group health insurance to the unemployed, neither would they have a clear incentive for doing so. Furthermore, as with any innovation, spontaneous diffusion and adoption of such an institutional arrangement would probably take some time. For these reasons, governmental intervention of some kind may be appropriate to facilitate timely adoption of the concept—for example, "jaw-boning" or even legislation requiring it. In fact, such legislation has already been enacted in the state of Rhode Island.[10] It provides that "whenever the employment of an insured member of a group hospital, surgical, or medical insurance plan is terminated because of involuntary layoff or death, the benefits of such plan may be continued . . . for a period of up to 10 months from the termination date of the insured member. . . ."[11] The Rhode Island law includes other provisions:

> *The involuntary laid-off member or surviving spouse of a deceased member may elect to continue participation in the group plan within thirty (30) days after the member's involuntary lay-off or death. The involuntarily laid-off member or the surviving spouse of a deceased member shall be responsible for payment of premiums or subscription fees directly to the carrier of the surgical, hospital, or medical insurance plan, or the group plan's agent, throughout the extended coverage period, if the member had been covered under a group plan consisting of fifty (50) members or less. Those leaving group plans with more than fifty (50) members shall be responsible directly to the employer for payment of premiums or subscription fees (p. 2).*

This law was originally enacted for one year, from September 1, 1976 to September 1, 1977, but recently was continued indefinitely. Although no evaluation of experience with the law has been attempted, a spokesman for Blue Cross–Blue Shield of Rhode Island indicates that the plan is working out well and that reactions to it are uniformly favorable.[12]

Continuation of group health insurance through the former employer is not the only alternative for making group health insurance available to the unemployed, however. It is also possible that the pecuniary externalities can be internalized in the context of some other institutional setting. For example, the savings bank serves this function in Iowa. The savings banks in that state act as group health insurance purchase agents for their depositors in much the same way as employers do for their employees.[13] Such an arrangement not only makes group health insurance available to the unemployed but also makes it available to the self-employed and to other workers without access to group health insurance through their employment. Unfortunately, such arrangements are not widely available. Thus, it may be appropriate for government to furnish incentives for their development as well.

In Chapter 3 we estimated, using our most recent data, that between 875,000 and 1,071,000 workers and their families had lost health insurance at any one time because of unemployment at the peak of the 1974–75 recession. Our results in Chapter 4, from the same data source, suggest that either of the social innovations discussed above—(1) an option to purchase group health insurance from former employers, or (2) the marketing of group health insurance by savings banks and other institutions—might have reduced the health insurance loss to one-fourth of the magnitude actually experienced. That is, we estimate that 656,000 to 803,000 fewer workers would have lost health insurance because of unemployment. Furthermore, we now estimate that such reduction in health insurance loss would have increased social welfare by $69 million to $84 million, or about $105 for each unemployed worker regaining health insurance. In other words, it would have been worth that much to society to have had one of these institutional mechanisms available; it is our estimate of the cross-hatched triangular area in Figure 5–1.[14]

We wish to caution the reader that our estimates depend crucially on inferring from correlational analysis that the "price effect" is the primary cause of health insurance loss due to unemployment. Although we have presented some evidence for this view, it remains a hypothesis that requires further testing. The new law in Rhode Island provides an ideal natural experiment for such testing. The health insurance experience of the unemployed in that "experimental" state could be compared either to the experience of the unemployed in other "control" states without the law or to the data in this study.

THE IMPLICATIONS FOR
NATIONAL HEALTH INSURANCE

Although this has not been a study of national health insurance as such, it nevertheless has much to add to the ongoing discussion of national health insurance. The study has generated considerable up-to-date information on health insurance, not only among the unemployed but also among the employed. In general, our study has found a pattern of inequity and possible inefficiency in the present system of health care financing in this country. Chapter 3 indicated that the working poor have much less assistance with health care costs than the nonworking poor.

Primarily because of Medicaid, the nonworking poor pay only 32 percent of health care costs out of pocket while the working poor pay 54 percent of such costs; furthermore, the nonworking poor spend almost half again as much on health care as the working poor. Chapter 4 showed that a worker's probability of having health insurance depends substantially on the industry of employment, even after controlling for demographic and other relevant worker characteristics. That is, the provision of health insurance depends importantly on institutional arrangements unrelated to demand variation. It also depends on demographic factors unrelated to demand variation. For example, a self-employed worker is much less likely to have group health insurance than an otherwise similar nonself-employed worker. Furthermore, we found that a female or nonwhite head of household is less likely to have group health insurance than an otherwise similar male or white head of household.

We have shown both conceptually and empirically that reliance on the workplace as the predominant institutional mechanism for financing health insurance has led to some inefficiency and inequity. However, that is not to say the national health insurance would produce any less inefficiency and inequity. In the previous section, we recommend the development of alternative institutional arrangements for making group health insurance available to the unemployed. Our data suggest that such a social innovation would solve much or most of the problem of health insurance loss resulting from unemployment. Perhaps widespread marketing of group health insurance by savings banks or other institutions would also solve many of the problems for which national health insurance is designed. We only raise the question; it cannot be answered from the present study.

NOTES

1. HR 3208, introduced by James C. Corman (D–California), is a similar bill. Like S 496 it was to give the unemployed workers and their families up to one year of hospital insurance under Medicare. However, it proposed to finance the program through a new tax of 0.2 percent on payrolls.

2. Bentsen also introduced a counterpart (S 1213) to Rostenkowski's bill in the Senate.

3. Medicaid benefits are currently available to some unemployed workers in about half the states. In those states an unemployed father may become eligible for AFDC benefits—and thus for medical benefits as well—if he

has been unemployed for 30 days, has some previous work experience, and is not receiving unemployment insurance benefits. See Chapter 3.

4. HEW Secretary Caspar W. Weinberger used an even more conservative estimate that only 15 percent of the unemployed with prior coverage had continued group coverage. (*Health Insurance and the Unemployed,* Hearings Before the Committee on Finance, U.S. Senate, p. 41.)

5. Of course, it takes time to make some of these adjustments. Thus, this problem might not have been severe for the short-run proposed "emergency" health insurance legislation. However, any attempt to extend such legislation over longer periods would confront this problem.

6. We have used the PRICE coefficient from CHAS estimation of the demand for group health insurance by the employed (see Table 4-4). The implicit price elasticity of demand is -5.5.

7. Also see Feldstein (1972), Gramlich (1974), Marston (1975), and Hosek (1975).

8. The social cost of continuing health insurance to the unemployed might also include a surcharge for the alleged adverse selection of health insurance risks among the unemployed. However, the greater risk among the unemployed (if any) might also be included as part of the entire work-group's insured risk. Indeed this is more appropriate to the extent that unemployment is caused by essentially stochastic health problems.

9. Because the benefits of continuation would be received only by those who pay for them, no redistribution of income is implied—that is, our proposal would not promote any distributional equity goals.

10. 76-S 2037 Substitute "A," Rhode Island Senate, January Session 1976.

11. The Florida insurance commissioner issued a bulletin during the recession recommending that insurers make group health insurance available to former employees (*L&H Informational Bulletin* 75-5). In North Carolina an emergency meeting of insurance companies was convened (March 3, 1975) by the insurance commissioner "for the purpose of determining the impact of the economic recession on consumer life, accident and health and life insurance coverage of unemployed citizens of North Carolina." A task force was appointed and it recommended making group health insurance available to laid-off workers for a 90-day period.

12. Telephone conversation with Richard B. Wolfe, Blue Cross-Blue Shield of Rhode Island, June 12, 1977. Mr. Wolfe further reported that there had been some initial concern about the loss of individual health insurance revenue but that it had not turned out to be a problem. He agreed that a larger group enrollment might well compensate for any smaller reduction in individual enrollment.

13. Telephone conversation with Mr. Calloway, an attorney for the Health Insurance Institute of America, June 12, 1977.

14. The welfare loss is approximated as
    $$-1/2 * (Q_U'' - Q_U') * (P_{individual} - P_{group}).$$
    We have calculated from the *Source Book of Health Insurance Data 1975-76*, HIAA, that the average group health insurance premium is \$300 per year; because otherwise equivalent individual insurance costs about 70 percent more, we estimate $P_{individual} - P_{group}$ as \$210, equal to .70 times \$300. We have taken the estimates from the text for the magnitude of $Q_U'' - Q_U'$.

Appendix A
Modeling the Incidence of Unemployment among Household Heads

THE RATIONALE FOR INVESTIGATION

To assess the loss of health insurance due to unemployment in Chapter 3, it was necessary to ascertain the extent of health insurance among the unemployed both before and after loss of employment. Unfortunately, only the "after" information on health insurance coverage is available. Thus, we assume that "before" information can be approximated from the coverage of those employed workers most likely to become unemployed—that is, those workers "at risk" of unemployment. These at-risk workers had to be identified, and in this Appendix we develop a model for that purpose. That is, we develop a model for projecting the expected duration (in weeks per year) of unemployment among household heads,[1] and thereby identify workers with the greatest expectation of unemployment. (Unemployment is defined as time spent without a job, either on layoff or looking for work.)

First, we discuss the theoretical determinants of unemployment; next, we develop empirical or operational specifications for modeling these determinants; and third, we report and discuss the findings.

A CONCEPTUAL PERSPECTIVE ON THE DETERMINANTS OF UNEMPLOYMENT AMONG HOUSEHOLD HEADS

The existing theory of unemployment is not well developed in view of the attention it has received. It tends to be fragmentary and mechanis-

117

tic. For example, it is customary to distinguish "frictional," "cyclical," and "structural" unemployment without any attempt to integrate these constructs into a general theory of unemployment. Similarly, it is common to analyze the probability of unemployment and the duration of unemployment separately even though the two depend on one another: the probability of unemployment may depend substantially upon the expected duration of unemployment, and vice versa. Moreover, Feldstein (1975, 1976) has shown that the usual distinction between "quits" and "layoffs" is not fully valid. Because workers often remain with the same employer through several spells of unemployment, the frequency and duration of temporary layoffs can be regarded as part of the total package of compensation and conditions, suggesting that layoffs are partly voluntary.

A more general or comprehensive conceptualization is needed to provide direction to the analysis of unemployment. Though this goal is beyond our purpose, the broad conceptual role of unemployment can be more correctly understood in the context of conventional supply and demand analysis. Our discussion is only exploratory and preliminary, but we hope that it may at least provide impetus to further investigation of the supply-demand approach.

To begin our model, we shall assume that Figure A-1 portrays the labor market. The S_* curve represents what the long-run supply of labor would be if "job search" were costless to the worker, and the D_* curve represents what the long-run demand for labor would be if "worker recruitment" were costless to the employer. Realistically, of course, neither job search or worker recruitment is costless. Both entail monetary, opportunity, and psychic costs. Thus, at N_*, the actual labor cost is not w_* but $w_* + c_D$, where c_D represents the recruitment or hiring cost to the employer—including the costs of advertising, processing the applicants, and training the new hiree for a specific position. Similarly, the wage return to the employee is $w_* - c_s$, where c_S represents the search cost to the employee—primarily the income foregone while unemployed. For this reason the actual supply and demand curve—S_{actual} and D_{actual}—diverge from S_* and D_*, as shown in Figure A-1,[2] and determine an equilibrium level of employment, N_{actual}, that is less than N_*.

We now assert that $N_* - N_{actual}$ represents the "true" extent of unemployment in the sense that it is the maximum number of persons not presently employed who would be willing to work at any feasible wage level—that is, at any wage that satisfies both the supply and demand constraints. $N_* - N_{actual}$ is the theoretic construct that we wish to model, and

Figure A-1
The Labor Market

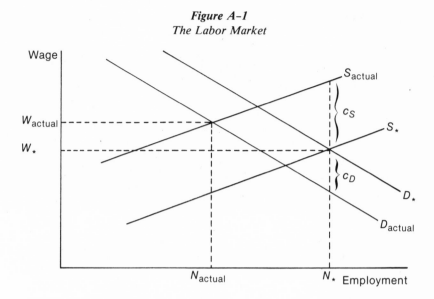

reported unemployment is merely a proxy for this theoretically appropriate variable—and a very imperfect proxy at that. Some persons who claim to be looking for work are not in fact doing so, or at least not searching for immediate (re)employment. Furthermore, some persons who would be willing to work at wage w_* may be discouraged by the search costs and drop out of the labor force, thus not being counted in the statistics on unemployment.

The magnitudes of c_S and c_D are not fixed but rather emerge from worker and employer optimization, respectively. The worker seeks to maximize the (present) value of working, trading off present employment for the prospect of more lucrative future employment.[3] As the employee's marginal net benefit of continuing with an employer decreases or as the marginal net benefit of job search increases, the magnitude of c_S increases.[4] The situation is analogous in determining c_D. The employer seeks to maximize the (present) value of worker productivity, trading off labor productivity in the present for the prospect of more productive labor in the future.[5] As the marginal net benefit of continuing an employee decreases, or as the marginal net benefit of recruiting increases, the magnitude of c_D increases. The converse is likewise true.

In this appendix we will use a "reduced-form" equation to model the personal and socioeconomic determinants of c_S and c_D—that is, to explain what causes the supply and demand curves to diverge in systematically different ways for different kinds of persons, resulting in systematically different expectations of unemployment. In a sense we are modeling those factors which determine the distribution of unemployment, given the overall level of unemployment.[6] The level of unemployment is also determined by such factors as uncertainty, seasonality, cyclical and other fluctuations in product demand, and public monetary and fiscal policy, as well as worker characteristics.

A person's relative expectation of unemployment thus depends on the magnitudes of c_S and c_D in Figure A-1—respectively, the cost of job search to the employee and the cost of hiring to the employer. Several worker characteristics may influence the magnitudes of these costs and thereby determine the expectation of unemployment, taking the overall level of unemployment as given. Our study does not include all workers, but is limited to household heads because the "household" is the unit of analysis in Chapter 3. This restriction vastly simplifies the behavioral context of unemployment analysis. Because household heads tend to be either nonmembers or full-time members of the labor force, the findings are less "contaminated" by entry to and exit from the labor force or by the "discouraged worker" phenomenon than they would be if we included all workers.

Education. Schooling is widely believed to make workers more efficient and productive. If education also enhances the efficiency of worker job search, the optimal level of job search investment (c_S) will be decreased—lowering the expectation of unemployment.

A more educated worker may also be more efficient at learning on the job. On-the-job training is often specific to a particular firm and increases a worker's productivity in that firm but not in any other.[7] Because the employer can appropriate part if not all of the return to such firm-specific investment in human capital, the profitability of retaining employees who have been so trained is higher, other things being equal, and the employer's optimal c_D investment is lower—implying a lesser expected duration of unemployment. To the extent that employees can appropriate part of the return to firm-specific human capital investment, the benefits to them of remaining with the employer are greater, other things equal, and the employee's optimal job search investment is less— also implying a lower expectation of unemployment.

Education may further lower the employer's recruiting or hiring cost c_D, and therefore decrease the expectation of unemployment if (1) technological change is labor-saving and (2) physical capital substitutes more perfectly for unskilled (less educated) labor than for skilled.

Age. Various arguments suggest that the expectation of unemployment declines with age. First, the job search cost c_S is predicted to be lower for older workers who often have acquired more specialized skills and therefore tend to search in more restricted labor markets than younger workers. Furthermore, to the extent that age is a proxy for experience with the labor market, an older worker may be more efficient at job search. For example, a younger worker may be less adept at evaluating employment prospects and therefore more likely to make a "mistake" by accepting a subsequently unsatisfactory job, necessitating a further search and increasing total job search costs. The limited labor market experience of younger workers likewise makes it difficult for an employer to evaluate a younger prospective employee and may lead to an analogous increase in the c_D hiring cost. Worker seniority provisions may also shift the burden of labor market equilibration to the young. And to the extent that age is colinear with duration of employment, an older worker is likely to have acquired more firm-specific human capital and, in consequence, to have a lower expectation of unemployment.

However, it may also be argued that the expectation of unemployment is higher for the oldest workers inasmuch as both employee and employer hiring cost investments must be amortized over a shorter time interval. Thus, the relationship between the expected duration of unemployment and age may be nonlinear, declining with age over some lower-age interval and increasing with age over some upper-age interval.

Race and Sex. Race and sex discrimination within the labor market implies that the burden of labor market equilibration is inequitably shifted toward nonwhites and women. The discriminating employer finds the benefits from continuing the employment of a nonwhite worker are less than the benefits from continuing employment for an otherwise similar white worker. This implies, as discussed above, that the c_D hiring cost—and therefore the expected duration of unemployment—is greater for nonwhites.[8] The same argument can be made with respect to female workers. Furthermore, the net benefits of continuing with an employer are lower for women for whom "homemaking" is a viable alternative, suggesting that the c_s search cost is also higher for the average female.

Marital Status and Number of Children.   A married worker, whose spouse is present, is said to have a larger "need" for income than an otherwise similar unmarried worker. Given the existence of imperfect capital markets and an unemployed worker's inability to borrow against future income, a worker with greater need is more likely to experience "financial hardship" while unemployed. This may be viewed as a psychic cost which increases the marginal cost of job search and reduces the marginal net benefits, thereby causing a decrease in the magnitude of c_S. The expectation of unemployment is consequently predicted to be lower for a married worker.

Because the "need" for income also varies directly with the number of children and other dependents in a household, the expected duration of unemployment is also predicted to vary inversely with a family size variable.

Wage.   The ultimate effect of wage upon the expected duration of unemployment is ambiguous.[9] A higher wage may either increase or decrease the expectation of unemployment, depending on the relative importance of opposing influences. For example, a higher wage means that it is more costly in terms of foregone income for a worker to be unemployed. This suggests that the optimal job search investment varies inversely with wage, and therefore that the expectation of unemployment is lower at a higher wage level. Similarly, c_S and c_D investments are reduced to the extent that the wage reflects a return to firm-specific human capital. However, the wage is also known to be correlated with the net worth of assets, an unobserved variable, and therefore may reflect an "income effect" in the sense that unemployment can be more easily financed by a higher wage, high asset worker. Both the worker's tangible costs of borrowing and intangible or "psychic" costs, associated with inability to borrow, are reduced, increasing the expectation of unemployment. Finally, a higher wage may itself, *ceteris paribus,* constitute compensation for the greater incidence of unemployment in some industries. (This last point is further discussed later in this appendix.)

Other Family Income.   Other family income—total family income less earnings of the head—is also an indicator of the need for income. To the extent that the family has alternative sources of income, the hardship costs of unemployment may be avoided, increasing the optimal level of job search investment and thereby increasing the expectation of unemployment.

Residence. Both employer and employee search are likely to be more efficient in a labor market with a higher density of workers and jobs. Job contacts will be less expensive because travel costs are lower. Furthermore, hiring is less likely to involve worker relocation with attendant "psychic" and monetary costs. Thus, we predict that the expectation of unemployment is lower in a larger community.

Occupation. The more skilled occupations are more likely to involve specific training and thereby to decrease the c_S and c_D investments, lowering the expectation of unemployment.

Industry. Variations in unemployment prospects across industries probably reflect seasonal factors and differential instability, cyclical and noncyclical, in the product markets. Durable manufacturing and construction, for example, are subject to greater demand variability; seasonality is more important in agriculture, forestry, fishing, and construction. These factors lower the profitability of uninterrupted employment and therefore increase the optimal level of hiring (and training) investment c_D. Furthermore, to the extent that industry of employment is not fully exogenous, it is probable that employees must be compensated in some way (such as higher wages) for the greater incidence of unemployment, shifting the burden of unemployment to the employer and accounting for a further increase in c_D. Of course, it is also possible that unemployment-prone industries attract workers with a stronger preference for leisure.

Class of Work. Self-employed workers are not eligible for unemployment compensation. Furthermore, the self-employed can more readily adjust the number of hours worked without becoming unemployed, increasing the total benefit from continued employment and reducing the job search cost. Thus, we predict that the mean job search cost will be less for the self-employed than it is for others, and that the expectation of unemployment will be lower.

Unemployment Insurance. Unemployment compensation reduces the employee's cost of job search and thus increases the net benefits of job search investment, increasing the total magnitude of c_s and increasing the expectation of unemployment.

Our basic conceptual view of the labor market has yielded a number of hypotheses about the effects of certain personal and socioeconomic characteristics on the expectation of unemployment. These hypotheses can be summarized as follows:

1. The relationship between the expectation of unemployment and age is nonlinear, declining with age over some lower-age interval but increasing with age over some upper-age interval.

2. The expectation of unemployment varies inversely with education.

3. The expectation of unemployment is higher for nonwhites and for women.

4. The expectation of unemployment is lower for married persons.

5. The expectation of unemployment varies inversely with the number of children.

6. The expectation of unemployment varies with the worker's wage, but the nature of such variation is ambiguous.

7. The expectation of unemployment varies directly with other family income.

8. The expectation of unemployment is lower in larger communities.

9. The expectation of unemployment is lower in more skilled occupations.

10. The expectation of unemployment varies systematically with industry of employment. In particular, the probability of unemployment is higher in those industries with greater seasonality and demand variability.

11. The expectation of unemployment is lower for self-employed workers.

12. The expectation of unemployment varies directly with the generosity of unemployment compensation.

As usual, our conceptual development has been guided, and limited, by the availability of data to examine the hypotheses; it is likely that we have failed to consider some variables that are potentially important determinants of unemployment. Nevertheless, we will estimate the simple model that emerges from our discussion and thereby give at least a partial explanation of unemployment among household heads. However, these results should not be viewed as a serious test of our conceptual model. The hypotheses we have generated are not conspicuously different from those which derive from alternative models—for example, the Markovian model of James Hosek. No doubt further refinement of the general conceptual approach would lead to hypotheses that better discriminate among alternative models of unemployment. Meanwhile, it is useful to demonstrate that unemployment can be understood, at least as well, in the context of a conventional supply and demand approach.

SPECIFICATION OF THE EMPIRICAL ANALYSIS

In this section we attempt to operationalize the conceptual model. In particular, we specify the estimation of a reduced-form type relationship between the expected duration of unemployment and the various personal and socioeconomic characteristics that we identified as determinants of unemployment.

The relationship between unemployment of the household head and his (or her) characteristics can be thought of as in equation A-1:

DUR = F (EDUC, AGE, AGESQ, RACE, SEX, MSTAT, NCHILD,
WAGE, OTHINC, RES1, RES2, OCC1–OCC4, IND1–
IND8, CLASS, UCSTATE)[10]   (Eq. A-1)

where the dependent variable DUR is the actul duration of unemployment (in weeks per year) and the independent variables are the characteristics of the household head, as defined in Table A-1. The DUR dependent variable is a limited dependent variable, with observations clustered at the limit—in particular, those persons not unemployed in a given year will have DUR equal to zero. The classical regression model is thus not appropriate (Goldberger 1964, pp. 251–255). We have instead employed a variation of the twin linear probability function (see Goldberger) to estimate equation A-1.[11] In particular, we used a Probit equation (see pp. 62–64) to model a dichotomous variable WS, equal to 0 if DUR = 0 and equal to 1 if DUR>0. Then, restricting the sample to those with DUR>0, we fit an ordinary least squares (OLS) regression with DUR as the dependent variable.[12] The first function, the Probit function, estimates the probability that DUR exceeds zero. The second function estimates the magnitude of DUR, given that it exceeds zero. The two results are then multiplied to obtain the unconditional expectation of unemployment:

$$DUR = \text{Prob } \{DUR>0\} \cdot E \{DUR/DUR>0\}$$ (Eq. A-2)

We also estimated the *WS* function using OLS, the usual twin probability approach.

Table A-1 Identification of Variables

DUR—Duration of unemployment, in weeks, April 1974–March 1975

EDUC—Years of schooling completed (a proxy for education)

AGE—Age in years

AGESQ—Age squared

RACE—Dummy variable indicating race
  0—white
  1—nonwhite

SEX—Dummy variable indicating sex
  0—male
  1—female

MSTAT—Dummy variable indicating marital status
  0—not married
  1—married, spouse present

NCHILD—Number of children under 18

WAGE—Proxy for head's wage (annual earnings divided by weeks
  worked)

OTHINC—Other family income (total annual family income less earnings of
  the head)[a]

Residence[b]
(Dummy variables)

RES1—SMSA, central city

RES2—Non-SMSA

Occupation[c]
(Dummy variables)

OCC1—Clerical and sales workers

OCC2—Blue-collar workers

OCC3—Service workers

OCC4—Farm workers

Industry[d]
(Dummy variables)

IND1—Agriculture and private household

IND2—Mining

IND3—Construction

IND4—Manufacturing

IND5—Transportation and public utilities

Table A–1 *continued*

IND6—Wholesale and retail trade

IND7—Finance, insurance, and real estate

IND8—Public administration

CLASS—Dummy variable indicating class of work.

       0—not self-employed

       1—self-employed

UCSTATE—Average weekly benefit paid by state unemployment insurance, 1974[e]

Source: All variables, except UCSTATE—1975 Current Population Survey; UCSTATE—*Unemployment Insurance Statistics,* U.S. Department of Labor (March 1975), p. 65.

[a]Unemployment compensation paid to the head is also excluded.

[b]SMSA, noncentral city is omitted.

[c]Professional and technical workers is omitted.

[d]Miscellaneous services is omitted.

[e]State of residence could not be uniquely identified from the 1975 Current Population Survey. States were grouped into 23 clusters of contiguous states and UCSTATE represents the mean value for each cluster.

The Annual Demographic File of the 1975 Current Population Survey was the data base. Work experience is reported from this source for the calendar year from April 1974 to March 1975. This interval spans the economic contraction that began slowly in late 1973, gained momentum in late 1974, and bottomed out in early 1975 when unemployment reached postwar heights. During this one-year period, unemployment went from 5 percent to 8.5 percent, and averaged 6.4 percent.[13] The 1975 CPS included over 22,000 households in which the head had been a full-year member of the labor force—either employed, laid off, or looking for work. For economy we used a 10 percent random sample of this population to estimate both the Probit and OLS probability functions. However, all unemployed heads were used in estimating the OLS duration equation.

Our operationalization of the conceptual model is imperfect because of the brief time covered by the data. Ideally, the model should have been estimated from data spanning a broader and more representative time interval, such as a panel of CPS data. This would avoid bias resulting from the unique attributes of any single-year period.[14]

RESULTS AND DISCUSSION

The results of estimation, both Probit and OLS probability equations as well as the duration equation, are shown in Table A-2. All three equations yielded highly significant relationships and the hypothesis of no relationship between the dependent variable and the independent variable list (that is, $b_1 = b_2 = \cdots = b_{25} = 0$) can be rejected at better than the .001 level in each case.[15] Fourteen of the 25 independent variables were significant at the .10 level or better in the Probit probability equation; 16 were that significant in the OLS probability equation; and 15 were significant in the duration equation.

Because of the nonlinear transformation involved in Probit analysis (see Chapter 4), the quantitative importance of the Probit coefficients cannot be easily discerned from the parameter estimates reported in Table A-2. For this reason the estimated Probit model has been used to predict the effect of variation in each of the independent variables on the probability of unemployment, taking other variables at their mean values. For example, it is shown in Table A-3 that as years of schooling (EDUC) rise from 8 to 12 years, the probability of unemployment declines by 3 percentage points. It is also shown that employment in the construction industry (IND3) is associated with a 12.7 percentage point greater probability of unemployment than employment in the miscellaneous services industry. To faciliate comparison of the Probit and OLS models, the OLS-estimated effects are also shown in Table A-3.[16]

The Probit and OLS techniques gave qualitatively similar results. Except for one highly insignificant variable (OCC3), the signs of the coefficients were the same in both models. Even the levels of significance were remarkably similar and, except for RACE and IND1, the same variables were significant in both relations. Thus, the two models do not have differential implications with respect to testing the hypotheses set forth in the first section of the appendix. Although the two models do estimate quantitatively different effects for at least some variables (such as RACE, WAGE, OCC4, and IND3), the magnitudes are still approximately similar.

Though we have estimated the unemployment probability and conditional duration relationships separately, it may not be appropriate to examine them in isolation. As suggested earlier, the probability and duration of unemployment are not likely to be independent of one another. Thus, a more fully specified structural model is needed to estimate these relationships without risk of simultaneous-equations bias.

Table A-2 The Determinants of Unemployment Among Household Heads, 1974–75

Independent Variable	Probability Equation (N = 5,897)		Duration Equation (N = 2,215)
	Probit Model	OLS Model	
Constant	.324 (+.844)	.290* (4.47)	24.6* (6.94)
AGE (age)	−.0386* (−2.97)	−.0075* (−3.52)	−.391* (−3.08)
AGESQ (age squared)	.000312* (2.05)	.0000633* (2.58)	.00541* (3.54)
EDUC (education)	−.0427* (−4.43)	−.00679* (−4.26)	−.364* (4.17)
RACE (nonwhite)	.122 (1.55)	.0265* (1.86)	.946 (1.34)
SEX (female)	−.0838 (−.529)	−.0135 (−.480)	.225 (.145)
MSTAT (married)	−.247* (−1.81)	−.0432* (−1.78)	−2.54* (−1.90)
NCHILD (number of children)	−.00139 (−.0747)	−.00069 (0.226)	.426* (2.45)
WAGE (earnings per week employed)	−.000600* (−2.80)	−.000058* (−1.92)	.00700* (4.23)
OTHINC (other family income)	.00000211	.000000233	.000149*
Residence			
RES1 (central city, SMSA)	.0695 (1.16)	.0105 (1.07)	1.28* (2.23)
RES2 (non-SMSA)	−.0139 (−.237)	−.00156 (−.164)	1.64* (2.85)
Occupation			
OCC1 (clerical and sales)	.117 (1.30)	.013 (.968)	−1.78* (−1.77)
OCC2 (blue collar)	.281* (3.81)	.0425* (3.69)	−.944 (−1.18)
OCC3 (service)	.0302 (.281)	−.00245 (−.142)	−1.90* (−1.78)
OCC4 (farm)	−.482* (−1.87)	−.104* (−2.23)	−3.38 (−1.34)

Table A–2 *continued*

Industry

IND1 (agriculture and private household)	.297 (1.44)	.0838* (2.02)	−.350* (−.190)
IND2 (mining)	.189 (.946)	.0381 (1.02)	−6.04* (−2.73)
IND3 (construction)	.606* (6.51)	.162* (9.50)	−2.81* (−3.14)
IND4 (manufacturing)	−.204* (−2.50)	−.0333* (−2.60)	−5.12* (−6.20)
IND5 (transportation and public utilities)	−.228* (−2.13)	−.0393* (−2.34)	−3.64* (03.31)
IND6 (wholesale and retail trade	−.0919 (1.07)	−.0153 (−1.12)	−1.07 (−1.22)
IND7 (finance, insurance, and real estate)	−.285* (1.90)	−.0377* (−1.81)	.128 (.0746)
IND8 (public administration)	−.319* (2.56)	−.0437* (−2.50)	−.362 (−.231)
CLASS (self-employed)	−.237* (−2.56)	−.0367* (−2.65)	−.618 (−.633)
UCSTATE (unemployment compensation)	.0130* (3.74)	.00209* (3.75)	.0520 (1.58)
Coefficient of determination (R^2)		.075	.073
Corrected coefficient of determination		.071	.062
F-ratio		18.3	6.9
Log likelihood ratio	−201		
Significance level of F-ratio or log likelihood ratio	<.001	<.001	<.001

Note: t statistics in parentheses.

*Significant at the .10 level or better.

Table A-3 Simulating the Effect on Unemployment Probability of Variation in the Independent Variables

Variable Identification and Values	Effect on Probability of Unemployment (in Percentages)	
	Probit Model	OLS Model
Age (AGE)		
20	0	0
30	− 4.8	− 4.3
40	− 7.6	− 7.4
50	− 9.0	− 9.2
60	− 9.6	− 9.7
Education (EDUC)		
8	0	0
10	− 1.6	− 1.4
12	− 3.0	− 2.8
14	− 4.2	− 4.1
16	− 5.3	− 5.5
18	− 6.3	− 6.8
Nonwhite (RACE)	+ 1.9	+ 2.7
Female (SEX)	− 1.2	− 1.3
Married (MSTAT)	− 4.3	− 4.3
Number of children (NCHILD)		
0	0	0
1	0.0	− 0.1
2	0.0	− 0.2
3	− 0.1	− 0.3
4	− 0.1	− 0.3
Earnings per week employed (WAGE)		
100	0	0
200	− 1.0	− 0.6
250	− 1.4	− 0.9
350	− 2.3	− 1.5
500	− 3.5	− 2.3
Other family income (OTHINC)		
0	0	0
2,000	0.0	+ 0.1
4,000	+ 0.1	+ 0.1
6,000	+ 0.2	+ 0.2
8,000	+ 0.2	+ 0.2
10,000	+ 0.3	+ 0.3

Table A-3 *continued*

Residence		
SMSA-noncentral city (omitted category)	0	0
SMSA-central city (RES1)	+ 1.1	+ 1.1
Non-SMSA (RES2)	− 0.3	− 0.2
Occupation		
Professional and technical (omitted category)	0	0
Clerical and sales (OCC1)	+ 1.9	+ 1.3
Blue collar (OCC2)	+ 4.4	+ 4.3
Service (OCC3)	+ .4	− .2
Farm (OCC4)	− 5.4	− 10.4
Industry		
Miscellaneous services (omitted category)	0	0
Agriculture and private household (IND1)	+ 5.4	8.4
Mining (IND2)	+ 3.2	3.8
Construction (IND3)	+ 12.7	16.1
Manufacturing (IND4)	− 3.0	− 3.3
Transportation and public utilities (IND5)	− 3.0	− 3.9
Wholesale and retail trade (IND6)	− 1.3	− 1.5
Finance, insurance, and real estate (IND7)	− 3.6	− 3.8
Public administration (IND8)	− 4.0	− 4.4
Self-employed (CLASS)	− 3.2	− 3.7
Unemployment compensation (UCSTATE)		
40	0	0
50	+ 1.5	+ 2.1
60	+ 3.3	+ 4.2
70	+ 5.4	+ 6.3
80	+ 7.9	+ 8.4

The relationships were in fact estimated separately only to form the twin linear probability function and, from that, to estimate reduced-form effects on the (unconditional) expected duration of unemployment. The estimated reduced-form effects are shown in Table A–4. We obtained the estimates by multiplying the predicted probability of unemployment— Probit or OLS—times the duration of unemployment predicted for those actually unemployed. In this way we simulate the effect of variation in

Table A-4 Simulating the Effect on Unemployment Expectation of Variation in the Independent Variables

Variable Identification and Values	The Effect on the Expected Duration of Unemployment (in Weeks)	
	Probit Model	OLS Model
Age (AGE)		
20	0	0
30	− 0.91	− 0.86
40	− 1.35	− 1.34
50	− 1.49	− 1.53
60	− 1.49	− 1.49
Education (EDUC)		
8	0	0
10	− 0.33	− 0.32
12	− 0.62	− 0.61
14	− 0.86	− 0.89
16	− 1.06	− 1.14
18	− 1.23	− 1.37
Nonwhite (RACE)	+ 0.39	+ 0.53
Female (SEX)	− 0.17	− 0.17
Married (MSTAT)	− 0.86	− 0.91
Number of children (NCHILD)		
0	0	0
1	+ 0.04	+ 0.04
2	+ 0.08	+ 0.06
3	+ 0.11	+ 0.09
4	+ 0.13	+ 0.13
Earnings per week employed (WAGE)		
100	0	0
200	− 0.08	− 0.02
250	− 0.12	− 0.03
350	− 0.20	− 0.05
500	− 0.33	− 0.08
Other Family Income (OTHINC)		
0	0	0
2,000	+ 0.02	+ 0.05
4,000	+ 0.06	+ 0.08
6,000	+ 0.10	+ 0.13
8,000	+ 0.13	+ 0.16
10,000	+ 0.17	+ 0.20

Table A-4.   *continued*

Residence		
SMSA–noncentral city (omitted category)	0	0
SMSA–central city (RES1)	+ 0.27	+ 0.30
Non-SMSA (RES2)	+ 0.09	+ 0.14
Occupation		
Professional and technical (omitted category)	0	0
Clerical and sales (OCC1)	+ 0.11	0.00
Blue collar (OCC2)	+ 0.59	+ 0.56
Service (OCC3)	− 0.10	− 0.22
Farm (OCC4)	− 0.94	− 1.60
Industry		
Miscellaneous services (omitted category)	0	0
Agriculture and private household (IND1)	+ 0.77	+ 1.20
Mining (IND2)	− 0.21	− 0.29
Construction (IND3)	+ 1.85	+ 1.78
Manufacturing (IND4)	− 0.82	− 0.95
Transportation and public utilities (IND5)	− 0.67	− 0.84
Wholesale and retail trade (IND6)	− 0.28	− 0.33
Finance, insurance, and real estate (IND7)	− 0.54	− 0.59
Public administration (IND8)	− 0.69	− 0.70
Self-employed (CLASS)	− 0.52	− 0.61
Unemployment compensation (UCSTATE)		
40	0	0
50	+ 0.24	+ 0.34
60	+ 0.56	+ 0.71
70	+ 0.93	+ 1.09
80	+ 1.38	+ 1.49

each of the independent variables, again taking other variables at their mean values. For example, Table A-4 shows that as years of schooling (EDUC) rises from 8 to 12 years, the expected duration of unemployment is estimated to decline by 0.62 weeks in the Probit model and by 0.61 weeks in the OLS model.

It is similarly shown that employment in the construction industry (IND3) is associated with either a 1.85 or a 1.78 weeks longer expectation of unemployment than employment in the miscellaneous services industry. Although such magnitudes indicate the quantitative significance of the variables, the statistical significance of those variables is less easy to discern. In fact, the sample properties of the twin linear probability function are not known. Thus, it is not possible to make rigorous statements about the significance of the independent variables. More informally, however, it may be presumed that a variable is significant in the twin linear probability function if it is significant in either the probability or the duration equations, or both, and has the same sign in both. A variable is not likely to be significant if it is highly insignificant in both the probability and the duration equation.

Given that the Probit and OLS probability equations gave essentially similar results, it should not be surprising that the Probit and OLS variants of the twin linear probability function in Table A–4, incorporating the respective probability equations, also yield essentially similar results.

Age. We previously hypothesized that the expectation of unemployment decreases with age over some lower-age interval but increases with age over some upper-age interval. The findings in Tables A–2 and A–4 support this hypothesis. The age variables were significant in both the probability and duration equations and the coefficients have the same' sign; furthermore, the expectation or expected duration of unemployment is shown in Table A–4 to decline until the mid-fifties, and then to increase slightly.

Education. As predicted, an increase in years of schooling is associated with a significantly lower expected duration of unemployment.

Race. As predicted, nonwhites are found to have a significantly or near-significantly higher expectation of unemployment.

Sex. Our hypothesis that a female head of household will have a higher expectation of unemployment is not supported by the results. On the contrary, a female head is estimated to have a somewhat lower expectation of unemployment, although none of the coefficients even approach significance. This result may reflect the greater ease with which a female head can withdraw from the labor force. Unlike unemployed male heads, an unemployed female head may be eligible for and choose to receive AFDC. She can also marry and reconstitute the household with a male as the head.

Marital Status. We hypothesized that the expectation of unemployment would be lower for married heads. Our finding that marriage is associated with a significant reduction in the expectation of unemployment (almost a full week) supports this hypothesis.

Number of Children. Contrary to our hypothesis, an increase in the number of children leads to a slight increase in the expectation of unemployment. We cannot explain this finding.

Wage. Although both probability and duration equations gave significant coefficients, the coefficients were opposite in sign. Thus, it is not clear whether the composite effect, a nominal wage-related reduction in the expectation of unemployment, is significant or not. Recall that we did not state a specific hypothesis with respect to wage.

Other Income. As hypothesized, the expectation of unemployment is found to vary directly and significantly with other family income, although the effect is not very large.

Residence. We predicted that the expectation of unemployment would be lower in a larger community. This hypothesis was not entirely borne out by the results. Workers in SMSA central cities are seen to have greater expectations of unemployment than workers in either non-SMSA communities or SMSA noncentral cities. Furthermore, the differences are potentially significant.

Occupation. It was predicted that the expectation of unemployment is lower in more skilled occupations. Our results suggest that the expectation of unemployment declines in the following sequence:

1. Blue Collar (OCC2)
2. Clerical and sales (OCC1)
3. Professional and technical (omitted category)
4. Service (OCC3)
5. Farm (OCC4)

With the possible exception of farm work and a reversal in the order of service employment and the omitted category, we believe that the occupational skill level broadly increases in the same sequence and that the results tend to support our hypothesis. The low expectation of unemployment among farm workers may reflect extraordinary costs of job search in the sense that a job change in farming typically involves a change in residence as well. It may also reflect the general exclusion of farm workers from unemployment insurance coverage. In addition, farm workers may be more flexible in adjusting the number of hours worked, *ceteris paribus,* in which case underemployment is more likely than unemployment.

Industry. We hypothesized that the expectation of unemployment varies systematically with industry of employment and that the expectation of unemployment is higher in those industries with greater seasonality and greater demand variability. We found that after controlling for other differences, the expectation of unemployment did vary systematically with industry of employment and that it declines in the following sequence:

1. Construction (IND3)
2. Agriculture and private household (IND1)
3. Miscellaneous services (omitted category)
4. Mining (IND2)
5. Wholesale and retail trade (IND6)
6. Finance, insurance and real estate (IND7)
7. Transportation and public utilities (IND5)
8. Public administration (IND8)
9. Manufacturing (IND4)

These findings offer some support for our hypothesis. The more seasonal industries—construction, agriculture, and mining—have high expectations of unemployment. Furthermore, some of the less cyclical industries—transportation and public utilities; finance, insurance, and real estate; and public administration—have the lowest expectations of unemployment. However, the finding that manufacturing has the lowest expected duration of unemployment is unexpected.

Class of Work. As predicted, self-employed workers have a significantly lower expectation of unemployment.

Unemployment Insurance. It was predicted that the expected duration of unemployment would vary directly with the generosity of unemployment compensation. This hypothesis was very strongly supported by the analysis. We found that a $10 per week increase in unemployment compensation benefits increases the expectation of unemployment by as much as half a week.

Though many of the hypotheses in the second section of this appendix were supported by the estimation, other hypotheses were not supported and raise questions to be examined in subsequent research. In any event, we cannot construe the results as evidence for or against our conceptual approach as such since other theoretic models yield many of the same hypotheses. However, the modeling of unemployment expectation, consistent with the supply-demand conceptual view, yields somewhat different results than does the modeling of unemployment probability or the modeling of actual (conditional) duration of unemployment in isolation. For example, the wage coefficient is positive, and significant, in the probability equation; it is negative, and significant, in the duration equation; but does not have a major quantitative effect when both equations were combined in the twin linear probability function. Similarly, sign reversals occur with respect to a number of other variables, including IND7, IND3, OCC2, and OCC1.

CONCLUSION

To assess the loss of health insurance due to unemployment as we do in Chapter 3, we needed to ascertain the extent of health insurance among the unemployed both before and after loss of employment. Because only the information on health insurance while unemployed was readily available, we assumed in Chapter 3 that the information on health insurance prior to unemployment could be proxied from the coverage of those employed workers most likely to become unemployed—that is, those workers at-risk of unemployment. These at-risk workers must nevertheless be identified and this Appendix has developed a model for that purpose—a model for projecting the probability of unemployment among household heads and thereby identifying workers with the greatest probability of unemployment.

In developing our model, we gave some attention to the theory of unemployment and recommend a view that tends to emphasize the conventional supply-demand nexus. Although we believe this approach to be superior a priori, the operational implications that emerge from it are not particularly different from those derived from other theoretic models. We hope that further refinement of our general conceptual approach will lead to hypotheses that better discriminate between it and alternative models of unemployment.

The operationalization of the model involved taking the actual duration of unemployment in a specific year as the dependent variable. However, because classical linear regression is not appropriate for such a limited dependent variable, with observations clustered at the limit, we used a variant of the twin linear probability function—one using the Probit model to estimate the probability equation—to estimate the overall model. We also estimated the basic model by the standard twin linear probability function—one using OLS to estimate the probability function. Because the results were substantially similar in the two estimations, the more convenient OLS version was used in Chapter 3 to identify the at-risk workers.

NOTES

1. The household is the unit of analysis in Chapter 3.

2. The search costs are arbitrarily assumed to be constant at all levels of employment. It seems likely, however, that both employer and employee search costs vary directly with the wage level—that is, c_s increases with N and that c_D decreases with N.

3. This extends George J. Stigler's analysis of search behavior (1961) in which the unemployed worker samples job offers until he finds one that exceeds his optimal reservation wage. See Lippman and McCall (1976) for a survey of the more recent, extensive literature on job search.

4. Merely awaiting recall from temporary layoff (or reemployment in season) can be an efficient job search strategy. A person need not be actively looking for alternative employment to incur job search costs.

5. See Lippman and McCall (1976).

6. It should be further understood that our purpose is positive or descriptive, not normative. We are not concerned, for example, with the relationship of N_{actual} to the optimal or "full employment" level of employment.

7. See Becker (1964), Oi (1962), and Parsons (1972).

8. Discrimination also impacts the overall demand for labor and may imply a lower wage, all other factors being equal. (Thus the wage variable is not fully exogenous.)

9. In a fully specified structural model, the wage would be endogenous.

10. Both an age (AGE) and age squared (AGESQ) are included to test for possible nonlinearity.

11. Although the Tobit model is now a more common procedure for this purpose, an efficient algorithm was not available at the time. Unlike Tobit, the twin probability approach takes no account of the error covariance between probability of employment loss and duration of unemployment.

12. Marston (1976) and Hosek (1975) estimate similar relations.

13. *Economic Report of the President* (1976), p. 199.

14. Marston (1976) and Smith, Vanski, and Holt (1974) have examined aspects of the cyclical pattern of unemployment.

15. Minus two times the log likelihood function is the goodness-of-fit criterion in Probit analysis. This statistic equals 403 in the estimated Probit probability model and is distributed as a chi-square with 26 degrees of freedom.

16. In the case of dichotomous variables, the OLS-estimated effect is the same as the coefficient.

Bibliography

Arrow, Kenneth J. *The Theory of Risk Bearing.* Chicago: Markham, 1971.

_____."Uncertainty and the Welfare Economics of Health Care," *American Economic Review* 53 (December 1963), pp. 941–73.

_____."Welfare Analysis of Changes in Health Coinsurance Rates," in *The Role of Health Insurance in the Health Services Sector,* ed. Richard N. Rosett. New York: National Bureau of Economic Research, 1976, pp. 3–23.

Auster, Richard, Irving Leveson, and Deborah Sarachek. "The Production of Health, An Exploratory Study," *Journal of Human Resources* 4 (Fall 1969): 411–36.

Becker, Gary S. *Human Capital.* New York: Columbia University Press, 1964.

Blair, Roger D., and Ronald J. Vogel. *The Cost of Health Insurance Administration.* Lexington, Mass.: D.C. Heath, 1975.

Brenner, Harvey. *Estimating the Social Costs of National Economic Policy: Implications for Mental and Physical Health, and Criminal Aggression.* A study prepared for the Joint Economic Committee, Congress of the United States, October 26, 1976.

Davis, Karen. "Achievements and Problems of Medicaid," *Public Health Reports* 91 (July–August 1976): 303–17.

Feldstein, Martin S. "The Importance of Temporary Layoffs: An Empirical Analysis," *Brookings Papers on Economic Activity* 3 (1975): 725–44.

_____."Policies to Lower the Permanent Rate of Unemployment," *Reducing Unemployment to 2 Percent.* Hearings Before the Joint Economic Committee, 92nd Congress, 2nd Session, 1972.

_____."Temporary Layoffs in the Theory of Unemployment," *Journal of Political Economy* 84 (October 1976): 937-57.

_____."The Welfare Loss of Excess Health Insurance," *Journal of Political Economy* (March–April 1973): 251-280.

Friedman, Milton. *A Theory of the Consumption Function*. Princeton, N.J.: Princeton University Press, 1957.

Fuchs, Victor R. *Who Shall Live*. New York: Basic Books, 1974.

Gibson, Robert M., and Marjorie Smith Mueller. "National Health Expenditures, Fiscal Year 1976," *Social Security Bulletin* (April 1977): 3-22.

Goldberger, Arthur S. *Econometric Theory*. New York: John Wiley, 1964.

Goldstein, Gerald S., and Mark V. Pauly. "Group Health Insurance as a Local Public Good," in *The Role of Health Insurance in the Health Services Sector*, ed. Richard N. Rosett. New York: National Bureau of Economic Research, 1976, pp. 73-110.

Gordon, Robert J. "The Welfare Cost of Higher Unemployment," *Brookings Papers on Economic Activity* 1 (1973): 133-195.

Gramlich, Edward M. "The Distributional Effects of Higher Unemployment," *Brookings Papers on Economic Activity* 2 (1974): 293-336.

Grossman, Michael. *The Demand for Health: A Theoretical and Empirical Investigation*. New York: National Bureau of Economic Research, 1972.

Hosek, James R. *Unemployment Patterns Among Individuals*. Santa Monica: The Rand Corporation, 1975.

"Jobless Medical Insurance," *National Journal Reports* 7 (March 29, 1975): 457-63.

Kaitz, Hyman B. "Analyzing the Length of Spells of Unemployment," *Monthly Labor Review* 93 (November 1970): 11-20.

Kmenta, Jan. *Elements of Econometrics*. New York: Macmillan, 1971.

Kolodrubetz, Walter W. "Group Health Insurance Coverage of Full-Time Employees, 1972," *Social Security Bulletin* 37 (April 1974):18-33.

Lippman, Steven A., and John J. McCall. "The Economics of Job Search: A Survey," *Economic Inquiry* 14 (June and September 1976): 155-89; 347-68.

Luft, Harold S. "The Impact of Poor Health on Earnings," Health Care Policy Discussion Paper 10, Harvard University, June 1973.

MacIntyre, Duncan V. *Voluntary Health Insurance and Rate Making*. New York: Cornell University Press, 1962.

Marston, Stephen T. "Employment Instability and High Unemployment Rates," *Brookings Papers on Economic Activity* 1 (1976): 169-203.

Mincer, Jacob. "Employment and Consumption," *Review of Economics and Statistics* 42 (February 1960): 20–26.

Modigliani, F., and R. Brumberg. "Utility Analysis and the Consumption Function: An Interpretation of Cross-Section Data," in *Post-Keynesian Economics,* ed. K. K. Kurihara. New Brunswick, N.J.: Rutgers University Press, 1954.

Mueller, Marjorie Smith. "Private Health Insurance in 1973: A Review of Coverage, Enrollment, and Financial Experience." *Social Security Bulletin,* (March 1976): 13–20.

Newhouse, Joseph P., and Charles E. Phelps. *On Having Your Cake and Eating It Too: An Analysis of Estimated Effects of Insurance on Demand for Medical Care.* Santa Monica: The Rand Corporation, R–1149–NC, April 1974.

Nordquist, Gerald, and S. Y. Wu. "The Joint Demand for Health Insurance and Preventive Medicine," in *The Role of Health Insurance in the Health Services Sector,* ed. Richard N. Rosett. New York: Bureau of Economic Research, 1976, pp. 35–65.

Oi, Walter Y. "Labor as a Quasi-Fixed Factor," *Journal of Political Economy* 70 (December 1962): 538–55.

Parsons, Donald O. "Specific Human Capital: An Application to Quit Rates and Layoff Rates," *Journal of Political Economy* 80 (November–December 1972): 1120–43.

Pauly, Mark. "The Economics of Moral Hazard," *American Economic Review* 68 (June 1968): 531–37.

Phelps, Charles E. *Testimony Before U.S. House of Representatives, Subcommittee on Public Health and Environment.* Santa Monica: The Rand Corporation, December 14, 1973.

_____. *Demand for Health Insurance: A Theoretical and Empirical Investigation.* Santa Monica: The Rand Corporation, R–1054–OEO, July 1973.

_____."Demand for Reimbursement Insurance," in *The Role of Health Insurance in the Health Services Sector,* ed. Richard N. Rosett. New York: National Bureau of Economic Research, 1976, pp. 115–55.

Rice, Dorothy P. *Estimating the Cost of Illness.* Health Economics Series, 6. Washington, D.C.: Government Printing Office, 1966.

Rossett, Richard N., and Lein-Fu Huang. "The Effect of Health Insurance on the Demand for Medical Care," *Journal of Political Economy* 81 (March–April 1973): 281–305.

Sloan, Frank A. Final Report to the National Center for Health Services Research, Contract No. HRA 230–75–0126, 1977 (forthcoming from Lexington Books).

Smith, Ralph E., Jean E. Vanski, and Charles C. Holt. "Recession and the Employment of Demographic Groups," *Brookings Papers on Economic Activity* 3 (1974): 737-58.

Stigler, George J. "The Economics of Information," *Journal of Political Economy* 69 (June 1961): 213-25.

Theil Henri. *Principles of Econometrics.* New York: John Wiley, 1971.

Thurow, Lester. *Investment in Human Capital.* Belmont, Calif.: Wadsworth, 1970.

U.S. Department of Labor, *Handbook of Labor Statistics, 1976.* Washington, D.C.: Government Printing Office, 1976.

U.S. Senate. *Health Insurance and the Unemployed,* Hearings Before the Committee on Finance. 94th Congress, First Session, March 7, 1974.

Waldman, Saul. *National Health Insurance Proposals: Provisions of Bills Introduced in the 93rd Congress as of July, 1974.* Social Securtiy Administration, Office of Research and Statistics, DHEW Publication (SSA) 75-11920, 1975.

Index

DATE DUE